# Journey to the Next World

## Understanding Death & Resurrection

---

*"There is no death. Only a change of worlds."*
- Chief Seattle, Suquamish Tribe (1853)

*"Life and death are one,
even as the river and the sea are one."*
- Kahlil Gibran

---

DR. HENRY G. COVERT

*Journey to the Next World:*
*Understanding Death & Resurrection*
by Dr. Henry G. Covert

Copyright © 2022
All rights reserved.

The Scripture texts used in this publication are from the New International Version of the Holy Bible, published by Zondervan Bible Publishers, Grand Rapids, Michigan.

Library of Congress Control Number: 2022945292
International Standard Book Number: 978-1-60126-821-1

Masthof Press
219 Mill Road | Morgantown, PA 19543-9516
www.Masthof.com

This book is dedicated to my mother, who somehow believed that her wayward and adventurous teenage son would one day become a pastor. This was realized when I was ordained at age forty-two, ten years after she departed for her heavenly home.

# Table of Contents

Introduction ....................................... vii

Chapter One: *Biblical Understanding of Death* ....... 1

Chapter Two: *Death and Resurrection of Jesus* ....... 28

Chapter Three: *Eschatology* ......................... 39

Chapter Four: *The Judgment* ......................... 44

Chapter Five: *Eternity with the Lord* ............... 61

Chapter Six: *The Spirit World* ...................... 71

Chapter Seven: *Affirmations of the Spirit World* .... 86

Conclusion ......................................... 112

Final Thoughts ..................................... 118

Scripture References ............................... 120

Resources .......................................... 123

# Introduction

The objective of this writing is to simplify an understanding of death and eternal life that is grounded in the Scriptures. It also serves as a starting point for those who desire to do more research on this topic. Although the mysteries of life and death are numerous and beyond our reach, it is possible to develop a certain level of comprehension that is rooted in history, extensive study, personal experiences, and the accounts of other people. In other words, it is a matter of compiling information and developing reasonable conclusions. However, one must realize that searching for truth has its limitations. Also, with any subject there is speculation, extreme thoughts, and deceptions that are put forth by individuals and groups.

Although death is as common as birth, people have a difficult time seeing the parallels, mainly that death is not the opposite of life, but rather part of it. While the birth of someone is celebrated, funerals bring sadness and a deep sense of loss. The thought of death unleashes many emotions, including anxiety and sometimes fear. But just as we prepare for a new physical birth within the family, we must also make preparation for our death and eternal future.

We make preparation for our physical death by purchasing insurance policies, cemetery plots, and writing our wills, but little time is given to spiritual preparation. I have known individuals who wrote their own obituary, making certain that all of their accomplishments were told. These same individuals, however, never mentioned God during their last days and hours. Although worldly preparations are necessary, they will not change our destiny. Most people claim to believe in an afterlife, but they deny it by neglecting spiritual truths and realities.

Someone asked Pope Benedict what he intended to do when he retired from the papacy. He responded by saying that he was going to prayerfully prepare for eternity. This brief statement is a witness of his faith, but it is also a message emphasizing that preparation for the next world is continuous. It is reported that someone asked Pope Francis if he ever thought about death. He responded by saying, "Of course, after all, there isn't much thread left on the spool." Regardless of one's age, the brevity and uncertainly of life should make everyone ponder their death and transition to the next life.

Disease, personal loss and death, are part of this life, and no one is excluded from these painful situations. The Church is given the mission of helping people prepare for such trying times. The apostles were Jesus' inner circle, yet they suffered intense suffering, persecution, and martyrdom. Rather than communicate superficial and simplistic responses for life's difficulties, the Church must be honest by conveying messages that are realistic. It is a wonderful feeling to engage in animate and joyful worship, but the struggles of life must be addressed by Christian communities. The objective of ministry is to help people develop a depth of understanding and faith that will enable them to prayerfully endure their suffering in faith.

Jesus told His apostles, "In the world you will have troubles. But take heart! I have overcome the world." (John 16:33) To suggest that our faith will somehow remove us from trials is not biblical. The question is not whether the trials will come, but rather how we will respond to them. Will it be in faith and perseverance or in anger? We live in a broken world, and we were not promised a trouble-free life. But we were promised divine grace to strengthen and sustain us through our earthly journey. Paul tells us that in Christ we become more than conquerors, meaning that, although our path is difficult, we grow through tribulation.

Around 935 B.C., King Solomon wrote that there is a time for everything and a season for every activity under heaven, including a time to be born and a time to die. (Ecclesiastes 3:1-2) Many books and articles have been written about death and the realm beyond this life. After all, who is not curious and concerned about their death and the realities leading to eternal life. This life is the only one that we know, and there is anxiety about what happens next. How will we die and at what age? What will we feel at the time of death, and will our soul instantly travel to another place? If this is true, will it be our final destination? When pondering life after death there are so many unanswered questions. One must conclude, however, that throughout history most people have believed in some manner of afterlife.

The author Victor Hugo (1802-1885) wrote about his own death when he said:

> When I go down to the grave I can say like so many others that I have finished my day's work. But I cannot say that I have finished my life. My day's work will begin again the next morning. The tomb is not a blind alley, but rather a thoroughfare. It closes on the twilight, and it opens on the dawn.

Henry van Dyke was an American author, educator, diplomat, and clergyman. Concerning death, he wrote:

> What is dying? I am standing on the seashore, a ship sails in the morning breeze and starts for the ocean. She is an object of beauty, and I stand watching her until at last she fades on the horizon. Then someone at my side says, "She is gone." Gone where? Gone from my sight, that is all. She is just as large in the masts, hull and spars, as she was when I saw her, and just as able to bear her load of living freight to her destination. The diminished size and total loss of sight is in me, not in her. And just at the moment when someone at my side says, "She is gone," there are others who are watching her coming, and other voices take up the glad shout: "There she comes!" And this is dying.

Those who have experienced near-death experiences resulting from some manner of medical trauma, have reported their feelings and sensations, as well as what they heard and saw. Their glimpse of the afterlife, although challenged by critics, have revealed similar experiences. Many of these individuals report moving through a tunnel and gravitating toward a bright light. In some cases, the person has encountered deceased relatives and friends or saw heavenly beings. The one theme that seems to be common are the feelings of euphoria and overwhelming love and peace.

While critics deny any of this as being true, scientific and medical communities point to neurological reasons for these experiences. There are some physicians who believe that certain medications are contributing factors. I am not qualified to comment on medical beliefs. This book is based upon an understanding of the Scriptures and my ministries to the dying. My intention is simply to report what I have learned and experienced in thirty-five years of being a pastor and state prison chaplain.

## PERSONAL BACKGROUND

To provide a foundation for this book, it is important that I share a brief outline of my background. Upon graduating from high school in Philadelphia, I enlisted in the Navy where I was a nuclear weapons instructor and an ordnance specialist on an aircraft carrier during the Cuban Missile Crisis. After my enlistment, including eleven months at sea, I was discharged and entered civilian life. The transition was difficult, and for a period of time I felt lost in an unfamiliar world. After several months of menial employment in Philadelphia, I decided to apply to a police department in Chester County, Pennsylvania. This decision led to nineteen years in law enforcement, which included patrol sergeant, county detective, state park ranger, and a state transportation agent. It was during this career that I developed an interest in both philosophy and theology. With veteran educational benefits, I entered Saint Joseph's University in Philadelphia on a part-time basis. This was followed by transferring to a Wesleyan College, where I obtained a bachelor's degree in Bible and theology.

Realizing my need for more education, I became a part-time student at Indiana Wesleyan University, receiving a master's degree in ministerial education. The graduate degree was obtained while pastoring my first church. It was a long and arduous journey up to this point. I recall having no intention of furthering my education except for denominational seminars.

After five years at my first church, I applied for the Protestant chaplain's position at Rockview State Prison in Bellefonte, Pennsylvania. The interviewing process was lengthy, involving all the department heads. They questioned me about my beliefs, philosophy of ministry, and how I would minster in a tense and diverse environment. There were also questions relating to my police background and the reasons why I left law enforcement to study for the ministry. A few of the interviewers wondered how the inmate population would react when they learned about my police background. Actually, I was wondering about this myself. I was put at ease when the superintendent said that I would be an asset in terms of adhering to security regulations. He also believed that my prior career would solicit respect from both staff and inmates.

After two weeks, I learned that I was accepted, and I was given a starting date. Within a few weeks, I entered the State Correctional Academy. As a police officer, I had graduated from the Pennsylvania State Police Academy, and now I was embarking upon more schooling in a much different career.

It was during my prison tenure that I again went back to school part time and obtained a doctorate in ministry degree from Pittsburgh Theological Seminary. This entailed taking all my days off and vacation time to complete my residency requirements. Fortunately, I was working on my dissertation while taking classes, which enabled me to complete my degree early. It was during this time that I became an adjunct lecturer in the sociology departments at both Penn State University and the Pennsylvania College of Technology. These part-time positions continued for ten years.

My doctoral thesis was titled *Ministry to the Incarcerated*, with an emphasis upon the stressors that impact inmate spiritual formation. After sending the manuscript to various publishers, I received a telephone call from Loyola Press in Chicago, Illinois, informing me that they decided to publish my writing. This book, which is still in print, contains my account of the first execution in Pennsylvania in thirty-three years.

The publication of my first book encouraged me to continue writing. I had no intention of writing this book, however, after doing a study on death and resurrection, combined with paranormal experiences and many hours with dying parishioners, I believe that my insights should be shared with others. At the end of my career, I had officiated at approximately one hundred funerals. All pastors know that funerals are not simply a service that is performed on a given day, but rather the many hours spent with the dying individual and their family, both before and after the death. These hours stimulate thought and form beliefs about our life journey.

My last ten years of ministry was in a small parish in State College, Pennsylvania, which was mostly seniors. It was a wonderful experience, being able to receive the wisdom and spirituality of those who had lived a long Christian life. This was followed by twelve years of pastoral supply for different denominations, which was an opportunity to learn different forms of worship and meet new people.

-Dr. Henry G. Covert

— CHAPTER ONE —

# Biblical Understanding of Death

**HEBREW BIBLE**

The Scriptures contain many reassuring words to comfort us as we contemplate the transition of our soul from this life to the next. Psalm Twenty-Three, penned by King David, is often read by clergy and lay people at worship and funeral services. This psalm, although seldom explained, is a message of comfort and hope. At the time of death, our soul—often referred to as our spirit—leaves our body to enter the spiritual world where both good and evil spirits dwell. David assures us of the Lord's protection as we are carried into God's presence. It is important that we examine this psalm:

> 1. The Lord is my shepherd. I shall lack nothing.
> 2. He makes me lie down in green pastures; He leads me beside quiet waters.
> 3. He restores my soul; He guides me in the paths of righteousness for his name's sake.
> 4. Even though I walk through the valley of the shadow of death, I will fear no evil, for you are with me. Your rod and your staff, they comfort me.

> 5. You prepare a table before me in the presence of my enemies; you anoint my head with oil; my cup overflows.
>
> 6. Surely, goodness and love will follow me all the days of my life, and I will dwell in the house of the Lord forever.

In this song of trust, David envisions the Lord as a shepherd and constant companion, who provides for and protects his sheep. (1)

The quiet waters and green pastures reflect a place of rest, peace, and restoration. (2)

The shepherd guides his sheep down the path of righteousness. This is the path that brings the faithful to God's special place. (3)

When we walk through the valley of the shadow of death we will not fear, for God is with us. The Jews saw death as a shadowy place, but this verse reveals a passing through the shadows. The shepherd protects his sheep with a rod that is used to fight off enemies, and he guides them with his staff. This is an assurance that enemies will not have power over us, for they will know that we are in God's care. Our anointing is symbolic of our healing and acceptance by the Lord, and the blessings bestowed upon us speak to God meeting all of our needs. (4-5)

David sees himself as a permanent recipient of God's kingdom and care. (6)

The Lord told Moses that he is the God of the living; of Abraham, Isaac, and Jacob. (Exodus 3:6) Jesus repeated this truth when He said to the Sadducees, who did not believe in the resurrection, "Have you not read what God said to you, 'I am the God of Abraham, the God of Isaac, and the God of Jacob?' He is not the God of the dead but of the living." When the crowds heard this, they were astonished at His teaching.

The Scriptures reveal a progressive understanding of death and resurrection. During early biblical times, the Jews believed that upon death everyone went to a place that they called *Sheol*, the origin of which is unknown. *Sheol* was a shadowy existence thought to be somewhere under the earth, but it was not associated with gravesites or burial locations. (Psalm 16:10; Jonah 2:2) Over time, the belief developed that *Sheol* had two separate dimensions, one for the righteous and the other for the unrighteous. This accompanied an understanding that God would eventually deliver the righteous from *Sheol*. In the Book of Daniel, which was written in the 6th century B.C., we read, "Multitudes who sleep in the dust of the earth will awake: some to everlasting life, others to shame and everlasting contempt." (Daniel 12:2) King Solomon assured the people that when the righteous die they have a refuge. (Proverbs 14:32) Job, which may be one the earliest books of the Bible, also alludes to a deliverance from death. (Job 19:25-27)

The Scriptures state that this earthly body is not the one that will be raised. In Ecclesiastes, King Solomon wrote that our earthly body will return to the ground from where it came, and the spirit returns to God who gave it. (Ecclesiastes 12:7) In this same context the apostle Paul wrote, "We know that if the earthly tent we live in is destroyed, we have a building from God, an eternal house in heaven, not built by human hands." (II Corinthians 5:1) Paul also wrote, "I declare to you brothers that flesh and blood cannot enter the kingdom of God, nor does the perishable inherit the imperishable." (I Corinthians 15:53)

During my ministry I was sometimes asked about my thoughts on cremation. Although my responses centered upon what is comfortable for family members, it is obvious that our earthly body must return to the dust. In fact, we know that this is a natural reality regardless of cremation. I understand the difficulty of letting go of the earthly body of a loved one, but it was intended to be temporary.

## NEW TESTAMENT

In Revelation we read, "He who has an ear, let him hear what the Spirit says to the churches. To him who overcomes, I will give the right to eat from the tree of life, which is in the paradise of God." (Revelation 2:7) This truth, given by the risen Christ to the churches of that time, is a message for us today. It is a theme that permeates the New Testament, which is the promise of salvation for those who have faith and walk in the Spirit.

Although the New Testament provides more understanding about death and the afterlife than the Hebrew Bible, there are similarities. In the New Testament, the Greek word *Hades* replaces the Hebrew *Sheol*. As in the Hebrew Bible, *Hades* had two places or locations, one for the righteous and the other for the unrighteous. To eliminate confusion, the word *hell* is the location in *Hades* for the unrighteous. This is also one of the words used when referring to the eternal destiny of the unrepentant. The Apostle's Creed states that after His death, Jesus descended into *hell*. Prior to the death and resurrection of Jesus, all departed souls went to one of the two locations in *Hades*. After the death and resurrection of Christ, the souls of the righteous no longer go to Hades. Instead, they are received into *Paradise*, which is also referred to as *heaven* or *Abraham's side or bosom*.

One of the two criminals who were crucified alongside of Jesus manifested faith, believing that Christ was divine. He said, "Jesus, remember me when you come into your kingdom." Jesus answered him, "I tell you the truth, today you will be with me in *Paradise*."

A graphic picture of *Paradise* and what occurs at the time of death is the story told by Jesus that is found in Luke:

> There was a rich man who was dressed in purple and fine linen and lived in luxury every day. At his gate, was laid a beggar named Lazarus, covered with sores and longing to eat what fell from the rich man's table. Even the dogs came and licked his sores. The time came when the beggar died, and the angels carried him to Abraham's side. The rich man also died and was buried. In hell, where he was in torment, he looked up and saw Abraham far away with Lazarus by his side. So, he called to him, "Father Abraham, have pity on me and send Lazarus to dip the tip of his finger in water to cool my tongue, because I am in agony in this fire." But Abraham replied, "Son, remember that in your lifetime you received your good things, while Lazarus received bad things, but now he is comforted here, and you are in agony. And besides all this, between us and you a great chasm has been fixed, so that those who want to go from here to you cannot, nor can anyone cross over from there to us." (Luke 16:19-31)

This picture of death is not about the rich versus the poor. Instead, it is rooted in one's lack of mercy for others. Since Abraham is considered the *father of faith* in the Scriptures, it is appropriate that Jesus would use him as an example of welcoming Lazarus into *Paradise*. Whether we use the word *Sheol* or *Hades*, there is a separation between the righteous and the unrighteous at the time of death.

This is an intermediate state for both the saved and the lost that will exist until the Second Advent of Christ at the end of the age. (Matthew 24:3; I Corinthians 15:23; II Thessalonians 2:3) The intermediate state is a place of joy, peace, and comfort for the righteous. It is the soul at rest in the Lord, where the worries, anxiety, and fear relating to the world does not exist. It is also a place where we no longer fear death. Although we are alive and conscious, there is no concept of time.

Some theologians believe that at the time of death the righteous will immediately receive their glorified and eternal body. Paul wrote about being unclothed when we die and longing for our heavenly body. He does not, however, state when we will receive our new body. He is speaking here about the intermediate state before the Second Advent of Christ. (II Corinthians 5:1-5) This understanding seems to be aligned with other Scripture, which makes a distinction between the intermediate state and the establishment of God's eternal kingdom when Jesus returns. Jesus said that in our final state we will be like angels. (Mark 12:24-27) John believed that when Jesus appears we will be like him. (I John 3:2) Whether it is our unclothed soul or new body, what matters is that we will be with the Lord before Jesus returns and after the Second Advent, which will bring this world to an end.

It is believed that our new body will bear a resemblance to our earthly one, thereby enabling recognition. The Scriptures and the near-death experiences of people seem to indicate this. Paul wrote, "What you sow does not come to life unless it dies. When you sow you do not plant the body that will be, but just a seed, perhaps of wheat or something else. But God gives it a body as he has determined, and *to each kind of seed he gives its own body.*" (I Corinthians 15:36-38) If not before, we know that during the Second Advent, the saints who have already died in faith will be clothed with a glorified body. The faithful, who are still living on earth at this time will be transformed, receiving their glorified body as they are raptured to join Jesus and the other saints in the air.

## PAUL'S EPISTLES

Paul was an educated Pharisee who, besides being a Jew, was a Roman citizen. While this was unusual, it spoke to his status as a Jew in the Roman world. He was a strict follower of Jewish civil and religious laws. He was influential and respected, and his interpretations of Scriptures were not challenged. Paul became the dominant theologian of the New Testament, whose missionary work and preaching was relentless.

Paul originally refused to accept that Jesus was the Messiah, and we learn of him traveling from Jerusalem to Syrian Damascus with a mandate from the high priest to seek out Jesus' followers. He intended to return them to Jerusalem for questioning and possible execution. While enroute, a bright flash of light shown around him, followed by a voice saying, "Saul, Saul, why do you persecute me?" When Paul inquired about the identity of the voice, the response was, "I am Jesus, whom you are persecuting." (Acts 9:1-6)

Paul was given instructions by Jesus to meet with other disciples and to preach the Gospel. What resulted was a life committed to missionary work and the establishment of Christian communities. He maintained contact with these groups through visits and letters, while continuing to preach throughout the region. He was eventually imprisoned in Rome and beheaded on the Apian Way when Nero was emperor. Since he was a Roman citizen, he was afforded an instant death, rather than the lengthy torture of crucifixion.

Prior to his execution, Paul wrote: "For me, to live is Christ and to die is gain. If I am to go on living in the body this will mean fruitful labor for me. Yet, what shall I choose? I do not know. I am torn between the two. I desire to depart and be with Christ, which is better by far." (Philippians 1:21-23) Paul's explanations on death and resurrection are more detailed than any other New Testament writer.

Paul's missionary journeys were far reaching and dangerous. Undoubtedly, there were times of discouragement when he needed the Lord's affirmation. As such, it is interesting to read his words regarding a supernatural experience that provided him with the strength needed to face his many challenges. In order not to boast about himself, he shared his experience in the third person.

> I know a man in Christ, who fourteen years ago, was caught up to the third heaven. Whether it was in the body or out of the body I do not know—God knows. And I know that this man—whether in the body or apart

from the body—was caught up to Paradise. He heard inexpressible things that man is not permitted to tell. I will boast about a man like that, but I will not boast about myself, except about my weaknesses. Even if I should choose to boast, I would not be a fool because I would be speaking the truth. But I refrain, so no one will think more of me than is warranted by what I do or say. (II Corinthians 12:2-6)

Many ancient cultures believed in three levels of creation, which are: the earth's atmosphere, the galaxies, and the place of the gods. Regardless how one defines *heaven* and its location, Paul emphatically states that he was taken to *Paradise*. Apparently, his experience was so sudden and traumatic that he was not certain if he remained in his body or if it was his conscious state that left his body. Paul's view of heaven's glory was overwhelming, affirming his faith and ministry.

This revelation may have resulted from a near-death experience that Paul had in Lystra, which is in present-day Turkey. Paul, along with Barnabas, went there a few times to preach the Gospel. On one trip Paul healed a crippled man who was unable to walk. After the healing a crowd gathered, believing that he and Barnabas were gods sent down in human form. The people, along with the priest from the nearby temple of Zeus, wanted to offer sacrifices to them.

While Paul and Barnabas were strongly refusing the people, Jews from Antioch appeared who convinced the crowd that Paul was spreading false teachings. This resulted with Paul being stoned, dragged outside of the city, and left for dead. Disciples came to his rescue, and after attending to him he recovered. The next day he and Barnabas left the city. (Acts 14:8-23) Although speculation, this may have been when Paul saw the vision of *Paradise*. It is certainly possible, particularly given the many reports today by people with near-death experiences. One thing is certain, Paul's insight into *Paradise* was not the result of medications or some manner of medical technology.

The early followers of Jesus had many questions relating to death, the end times, God's judgment, and eternal life. The Scriptures reveal that there were many misconceptions that were influencing the people during this time. Even the apostles and early disciples originally believed that the dead would be raised out of earthly graves. While the teachings of Jesus and Paul clearly dismiss this, the belief continues today. As we previously stated, many people do not want to think about their bodies returning to the earth. When I think about the millions of people who have died, with their bodies completely obliterated in wars, whether on land or at sea, I cannot imagine why this belief still exists. A prime example is when Nazi Germany exterminated millions of people. These and countless others over the centuries never had a gravesite.

In his epistles, Paul, provides us with insight into what happens at the time of death. While he admits that our knowledge is limited (I Corinthians 13:12), his understandings reflect the teachings of Jesus. In his first letter to the Corinthians, Paul laid the foundation for his teachings on the resurrection, using Jesus as our example. He wrote, "Christ has indeed been raised from the dead, the first fruits of those who have fallen asleep." (I Corinthians 15:20) He continued by saying that death came through one man, and the resurrection of the dead also came through a man. The former, of course, is a reference to Adam.

This is a starting point for Paul's theology, for if Jesus was not raised from the dead any teaching is meaningless. To the Christians in Rome, he affirmed the resurrection from the dead for all believers when he said, "If the Spirit of him who raised Jesus from the dead is living in you, he who raised Christ from the dead will also give life to your mortal bodies through his Spirit who lives in you." (Romans 8:11) This truth clearly connects our resurrection with the indwelling presence of the Holy Spirit.

The New Testament provides numerous proofs for the resurrection of Christ, including personal encounters in which Jesus appeared to His apostles and believers over a period of forty days. They saw the piercings in His hands, feet and side, which strengthened their faith and encouraged their preaching. Before His ascension, He commissioned them to preach the Gospel and baptize believers, promising them the anointing of the Holy Spirit. These promises began on Pentecost when the Holy Spirit came upon the apostles, providing them with the power and guidance for the many challenges that they would face. According to tradition, eleven of the twelve apostles were martyred for their faith and mission.

As Paul pondered this sinful world, he knew that his work for Christ was now his life. The resurrected Christ had clearly spoken to him. Jesus forgave Paul for his sinful zeal, and he was entrusted with the Gospel. I'm certain that Paul experienced disbelief as God placed His trust in him to be His voice on earth. Paul's first challenge was to convince the apostles that he had an encounter with Christ and was now a believer who could be trusted by them. This certainly did not happen overnight. After all, it was Paul who was intent upon arresting the followers of Christ.

When I sensed a call into the ministry I resisted, giving excuses why this was not my path in life. I questioned my feelings, and I had no desire to complete undergraduate and graduate degrees. I was married with a small child, and finances were strained. Also, I could not imagine carrying the burden and responsibility of a pastor. I was climbing the ladder in law enforcement, and the thought of leaving the security of my profession brought anxiety. We know that Paul did not resist the mission given to him by Jesus. He immediately gave up his prestige and security to do God's will, which was a journey that both changed the world and led to his martyrdom.

In his letter to the Corinthians, Paul responded to debates about the resurrected body. There was confusion relating to the physical body and the spiritual one. This led Paul to write, "The body that is sown is perishable; it is raised imperishable. I declare to you brothers that flesh and blood cannot inherit the kingdom of God, nor does the perishable inherit the imperishable." Paul continued by saying that both those who are alive on earth at the Second Advent and the saints who have died and are in *Paradise*, will undergo a bodily transformation. He also wrote, "Just as we have borne the likeness of the earthly man, so shall we bear the likeness of the man from heaven." (I Corinthians 15:35-54)

Paul emphasized again that our earthly body, although it was necessary and had its purpose, will not accompany us into our eternal future. He said, "We are always confident and know that as long as we are at home in the body we are away from the Lord. We are confident I say, and would prefer to be away from the body and at home with the Lord." (II Corinthians 5:6-8) Becoming a new creation in Christ is presently a spiritual transformation that will one day also be a bodily one.

In order to flesh out more detail concerning our death and resurrection, it is necessary to look at Paul's words in his letter to the Christians in Thessalonica:

> Brothers, we do not want you to be ignorant about those who have fallen asleep, or to grieve like the rest of men who have no hope. We believe that Jesus died and rose again, and so we believe that God will bring with Jesus those who have fallen asleep in him. According to the Lord's own word we tell you, that we who are still alive, who are left till the coming of the Lord, will certainly not precede those who have fallen asleep. For the Lord himself will come down from heaven, with a loud command, with the voice of the archangel, and with the trumpet call of God, and the dead in Christ will rise first. After that, we who are still alive and are left will be caught up with them in the clouds to meet the Lord in the air. And so, we will be with the Lord forever. Therefore, encourage each other with these words.
> (I Thessalonians 4:13-18)

We must note the words "God will bring with Jesus those who have fallen asleep." This is a reference to the righteous who died and are in *Paradise*. The "dead in Christ who will rise first" are the same saints. Both the words *sleep* and *rest* are employed throughout the Scriptures to describe the state of those who have died in the Lord.

When Lazarus died, Jesus told His apostles that Lazarus was not dead, but rather asleep. He said, "Our friend Lazarus has fallen asleep, but I am going there to wake him up." His disciples replied, "Lord, if he sleeps, he will get better." Jesus was speaking about his death, but his disciples thought that he meant natural sleep. (John 11:11-14) The raising of Lazarus from a tomb was intended to open the hearts and minds of the people, but his resurrection does not reflect how the dead will be raised at the end of the age. In Revelation we find a reference to the word *rest* within the context of death. "Then I heard a voice from heaven say, blessed are the dead who die in the Lord from now on. Yes, says the Spirit, they will rest from their labor, for their deeds will follow them." (Revelation 14:13)

Matthew tells us about a ruler who came to Christ stating that his daughter had just died. He believed that if Jesus simply touched her that she would live. When Jesus entered the ruler's house, there was a noisy crowd. He told everyone to leave, saying, "The girl is not dead but asleep." The crowd laughed at Him, but when she was brought back to life the news spread throughout the region. (Matthew 9:18-26) In his epistles, the Apostle Paul frequently referred to death as sleep. (I Corinthians 15:17-18, 51; I Thessalonians 4:15, 5:9-11) When referring to death, the words *sleep* and *rest* carry a similar meaning. With sleep comes rest, and this is the image that is intended. The world is filled with challenges and trials that bring anxiety. Since death removes us from the worries of this life, one can understand why biblical writers often used these words.

I recently read about the life of Soren Kierkegaard, who was a Danish philosopher, theologian, author, and social critic. He wrote numerous books on philosophy and religion, some of which are required reading in universities. Kierkegaard died in 1885 at the age of forty-two. He struggled as he questioned what it means to be a human being in this world. Just before he died, he told a friend that he hoped to be free of despair at the time of his death.[1]

I have encountered many situations in which people were tired and just wanted to fall asleep and enter a world of eternal peace and rest. My mother died at the age of sixty-three, after suffering from a stroke and heart disease. My father had passed away a few years earlier, leaving my mother lonely and despondent. During a visit she told me that she was tired and wanted to leave this world and be with the Lord. This was prior to my call to the ministry, and her words were upsetting to me. Of course, I now understand her feelings, especially since she was a woman whose life was rooted in faith. My mother longed to be with her Savior, just as the early Christians anxiously awaited the return of Jesus.

In his epistles to the churches Paul emphasized the glorious return of Jesus. He wrote the Thessalonians about his joy over their rejection of idols, unwavering faith in Christ, and how they eagerly awaited our Savior's return. (I Thessalonians 1:10) But to his coworker Timothy he said that one day people will reject the truth. He urged Timothy, saying, "In the presence of God and of Christ Jesus, who will judge the living and the dead, and in view of his appearing and his kingdom, I give you this charge: Preach the Word; be prepared to correct, rebuke, and encourage—with great patience and careful instruction. For the time will come when men will not

---

[1]  Clare Carlisle, *Philosopher of the Heart: The Restless Life of Soren Kierkegaard* (New York: Farrar, Straus, and Giroux, 2019), 248.

put up with sound doctrine." Paul continued by saying that people will turn their eyes away from the truth and believe in myths. Teachers will communicate what people want to hear to suit their own sinful desires. (II Timothy 4:1) Paul's predictions have always been a reality, but as we approach the last days, they have become more revealing. His words, "in view of his appearing and kingdom" manifest the urgency of preaching the Gospel and correcting false teachings. This is a message that the Church must act upon.

The author of Hebrews wrote, "Just as man is destined to die once, and after that to face judgment, so Christ was sacrificed once to take away the sins of many people; and he will appear a second time, not to bear sin, but to bring salvation to those who are waiting for him." (Hebrews 9:27-28) Again, we find the affirmation of Jesus' return, which will usher in God's kingdom.

In March of 2004, I preached the funeral sermon for a Lutheran pastor who was a close friend. As I reflected about the many trials that he had to endure in his lifetime, while still remaining faithful to his ministry, I recalled the following scripture written by Paul:

> Do you not know that in a race all the runners run, but only one gets the prize? Run in such a way as to get the prize. Everyone who competes in the games goes into strict training. They do it to get a crown that will not last, but we do it to get a crown that will last forever. Therefore, I do not run like a man running aimlessly. I do not fight like a man beating the air. No, I beat my body and make it my slave, so that after I have preached to others, I myself will not be disqualified for the prize. (Romans 9:24-27)

Paul knew the struggles and heartaches of life as he relentlessly faced the dangers and evil in the world. Yet, he stayed in the race giving all that he had, including his last breath for the Gospel. Paul knew that his Savior would return as promised. Whether he would be in *Paradise* at the Second Advent or still living in his earthly body, Paul was assured of his eternal future. As his life was nearing the end, he wrote Timothy, "The time has come for my departure. I have fought the good fight. I have finished the race and have kept the faith. Now there is in store for me the crown of righteousness, which the Lord, the righteous Judge, will award to me on that day—and not only to me, but to all who have longed for his appearing." (II Timothy 4:6-8) We are not promised a life without trials, but we are promised God's grace. Paul longed for the appearing of Jesus, for he was assured that it would bring him rest from his labor and eternal peace. This assurance comes to everyone who endures in faith.

Sometime around 537 B.C., the prophet Daniel reported seeing a vision of what appeared to be a person coming down from heaven. He referred to this individual as *one like a son of man*. Daniel's vision became well known with the people, who believed it to be a Messianic revelation. The Messiah was eagerly anticipated, and the Jews considered Daniel's words to be prophetic. It was understandable, therefore, that Jesus would refer to himself as the Son of Man. It was a title that the people knew, especially the religious leaders and teachers of the law. This is the vision that Daniel saw:

> In my vision at night I looked, and there before me was one like a son of man, coming with the clouds of heaven. He approached the Ancient of Days and was

led into his presence. He was given authority, glory and sovereign power; all peoples, nations, and men of every language worshipped him. His dominion is an everlasting dominion that will not pass away, and his kingdom is one that will never be destroyed. (Daniel 7:13-14)

Can you imagine seeing such a vision? Daniel said that he was troubled in his spirit and disturbed. When he questioned the meaning of the vision, he was given graphic images of tribulation, followed by victory for the saints and the establishment of God's kingdom. This vision unquestionably speaks to the Second Advent of Christ and the end times.

Important passages of Scripture relating to the Parousia are recorded in Matthew, where Jesus states that His return will be sudden and when least expected, thus emphasizing that we must be spiritually prepared. Jesus said, "For as the lightning comes from the east and flashes to the west, so will be the coming of the Son of Man." He compares it to the days of Noah and the flood, which came suddenly upon the people, leaving them no time to prepare. Christ reveals that His return will be preceded by deep distress and tribulation, followed by cosmic events. He spoke about the sun being darkened, the moon not giving its light, and the stars falling from the sky. Jesus said that this is when He will appear on the clouds with power and great glory, sending forth His angels to gather the elect. There is a debate whether Jesus' return will usher in a millennial kingdom on earth or whether it will only be for the rapture of the Church. The latter view is supported by New Testament teachings. What I find interesting is Jesus' acknowledgment that only the Father knows when these events will take place. (Matthew 24:36)

The "Parable of the Ten Virgins" found in Matthew presents a clear picture of being unprepared for Jesus' return. It speaks about ten virgins who were waiting for the bridegroom to appear in order to begin the festivities. To meet the bridegroom, there were two phases to Jewish weddings. First, the bridegroom went to the bride's home to receive his bride. This was when the religious ceremony occurred. The bridegroom then took his bride to his own home for the feast and celebration.

In our parable, there were ten maidens who were waiting for the bridegroom to appear so that they could enter the wedding feast, but they had no idea when he would arrive. Because the bridegroom was late, all the women fell asleep, and the lamps of five of them ran out of oil. They did not prepare like the other five maidens who took extra oil with them. When the bridegroom unexpectedly arrived at midnight, the women who had no oil hurriedly left to purchase more. When they returned, the door to the banquet was closed, and they were refused entrance.

This is how it will be when Jesus unexpectantly returns. Many people will not be spiritually prepared, and at His appearance it will be too late. Everyone should heed the words of this parable, for this is the time to live in faith and prepare our hearts. We are given the present to spiritually mature, thereby enabling us to enter the banquet feast. It is our faith in the midst of life's trials that make us worthy. Like a parent trying to counsel their children, the Lord continuously counsels us on the danger of rejecting His love and offer of salvation. The free will that enables us to accept God's love, however, also allows for resistance and self-destruction. Like the fork in the road, everyone is given a choice concerning which path to follow.

This is the time to make the choices that will determine our present and eternal future. We make daily decisions relating to the secular world and our personal life, but some people give little or no thought to their spiritual life. How many people, including professing Christians, are truly concerned about their inner life? Everything in this world, including our bodies, will be destroyed. It is the soul that lives forever and must be nurtured. How can we ponder eternity without being attentive to our inner life? Jesus called His disciples to take up their cross and follow Him, which means that they must live a surrendered life that is given to God and humanity. He said, "Whoever wants to save his life will lose it, but whoever loses his life for me will find it. What good will it be for someone if they gain the whole world, yet forfeit their soul?" (Matthew 16:24-27) This truth is clear, but does humanity listen? Didn't Jesus say that people have ears, but don't hear, and eyes, but don't see?

The Apostle John tells us about a time when many of Jesus' early followers left Him. It seems that He was not what they wanted Him to be. Rather than confronting their worldly concerns and Roman oppression, Jesus spoke about love, forgiving one's enemies, and an abstract kingdom. Many of His teachings were not what they wanted to hear. It became obvious that Jesus was not meeting their perceived needs. This story has a familiar sound, for it is the same plot that we find today.

As the departures were occurring, Jesus asked His apostles if they were also going to leave Him. Peter quickly responded by saying, "Lord, to whom shall we go? You have the words of eternal life. We believe and know that you are the Holy One of God." (John 6:66-69) Peter and the other apostles knew that Jesus was their hope. His words of truth pierced their hearts and transformed their lives. They were different people, who were not willing to return to their old life of bitterness and anger. It was God's love that changed them; a gift that they simply refused to abandon. They knew that they would confront persecution and possibly martyrdom, but their soul was more important than their body.

After His arrest, Jesus was taken before the Sanhedrin, where all the chief priests, elders, and teachers of the law came together to question Him. The high priest asked Him if He was the Christ, the Son of the Blessed One. Jesus' response was shocking to them. He said, "I am, and you will see the Son of Man sitting at the right hand of the Mighty One and coming on the clouds of heaven." (Mark 14:61-62) Mark recorded the anguish that resulted, stating that the high priest tore His clothing, accused Jesus of blasphemy, and pronounced His death sentence. The anger of the Jewish leaders centered upon Jesus' claim that He was the Son of God, which made Him equal to God.

When Jesus stood before Pontius Pilate, there was a brief, yet engaging dialogue. Pilate wanted to know who Jesus was and what He taught that incited the Jewish leaders. He was shocked that the leaders wanted a fellow Jew executed. Pilate asked Christ if He was a king. Jesus responded that He was, but that His kingdom was not of this world. He said that He came into the world to witness to the truth. Pilate, who by this time thought Jesus to be delusional, asked, "What is truth?" Little did Pilate know that he was looking at truth. This brief response was followed by the condemnation, torture, and crucifixion of Jesus. This was an historical and spiritual event that changed history and the lives of countless people.

When Jesus went to Bethany after Lazarus died, He was met by Lazarus' sister Martha. She told Jesus that if He had been there that her brother would not have died. Martha knew that Jesus had the power to heal the sick, but her brother was dead. What hope is there now? It seems that Jesus would simply be one of the mourners. But Martha still possessed faith, when she said to Jesus, "God will give you whatever you ask." Jesus then told her that her brother would rise again, to which Martha replied, "I know he will rise again in the resurrection at the last day." Then Jesus said to her, "I am the resurrection and the life. He who believes in me will live, even though he dies; and whoever lives and believes in me will never die." (John 11:1-44) Jesus brought Lazarus back to life, thus affirming His love, divinity, and power over death.

Revelation was written by the apostle John, who was banished to the island of Patmos. He was the only apostle who was not martyred. Revelation opens with the awesome appearance of a man dressed in a robe down to his feet and a golden sash around his chest. His head and hair were bright white, and his eyes were like blazing fire. His feet were like glowing bronze, and his voice echoed like the sound of rushing waters. In his right hand, he held seven stars, and out of his mouth came a double-edged sword. His face was like the sun shining in all its brilliance. John said that when he saw him, he fell at his feet as though dead, at which time the man placed his right hand on him and said, "Do not be afraid. I am the First and the Last. I am the Living One; I was dead, and behold I am alive for ever and ever! And I hold the keys of death and *Hades*." (Revelation 1:17-18)

This imagery is that of the Risen Christ. It reflects authority, power, and divinity. One can only imagine what John was feeling when he experienced this. What followed were Jesus' judgments of the Church during that time, insights into God's kingdom, and what to expect during the end times. In this final book of the Bible, we again find warnings that emphasize our need to be spiritually prepared for Jesus' return, when He will receive His Church, judge the world, and establish God's kingdom for the righteous. Throughout the Scriptures, God's love continuously calls us to repentance and salvation.

Luke gives an account of Jesus and His disciples entering Jerusalem during Passover. As Jesus approached the city, He wept, saying, "If you, even you, had only known on this day what would bring you peace, but now it is hidden from your eyes." (Luke 19:41-42) This reveals our Savior's sadness over being rejected, knowing what it meant for those who refused to believe God's message of forgiveness and reconciliation; the message that would bring them eternal peace.

In His attempt to warn the unrepentant of their plight, Jesus firmly said:

> When the Son of Man comes in his glory, and all the angels with him, he will sit on his throne in heavenly glory. All the nations will be gathered before him, and he will separate the people one from another, as a shepherd separates the sheep from the goats. He will put the sheep on his right and the goats on his left. Then the King will say to those on his right, "Come, you who are blessed by my Father, take your inheritance, the kingdom prepared for you since the creation of the world." (Matthew 25:31-34)

The separation of the saints from the unrighteous is a sad picture. It is no wonder that Jesus wept over the inhabitants of Jerusalem. He was sent by the Father to offer forgiveness and eternal life, but the people wanted to go their own way. Jesus preached the Gospel, healed the sick, and raised the dead, but they still rejected Him. Even after He was raised from the dead, the resistance did not change. But the Lord never withdraws His love from us. I once heard God referred to as the *"Hound of Heaven."* Although this is a strange description, it does communicate truth. The Scriptures speak about the final judgment, but we judge ourselves by refusing God's mercy and rejecting Christ as our Savior. It is disturbing to think that so many people refuse to acknowledge their need for God. Prayer and love are sometimes all that we can do for those who are blind to their eternal needs. God loves us equally, and it is not His will that anyone perish.

## WRITINGS OF THE APOSTLES

The Book of Acts, which records the acts of the apostles after the ascension of Jesus, was written by Luke around 61 A.D. In the first chapter, Luke recorded the ascension of Jesus. After telling the apostles that they would receive power from the Holy Spirit, Jesus was lifted up to heaven in their view. They saw Him rise until a cloud hid Him from their sight. Luke wrote, "They were looking intently up into the sky as he was going, when suddenly two men dressed in white appeared beside them who said, 'Men of Galilee, why do you stand here looking into the sky? This same Jesus who has been taken from you into heaven, will come back in the same way you have seen him go into heaven.'" (Acts 1:7-11)

Can you imagine how shocking it was to witness Jesus rising into the heavens? By now they believed that He was the Messiah, but I'm certain that this event was difficult to process. His teachings and healing ministry certainly bore witness to His claims. Then, there was Jairus' daughter and Lazarus whom He raised from the dead. However, it was Jesus' resurrection and ascension that sealed any doubt.

After this event, the apostles pondered His words and promises, including what He told them about *Paradise* and the Kingdom of God. Although they previously wanted to believe Him, they were now certain that everything He shared was true. This confirmation, combined with the power of the Holy Spirit, gave them the strength to preach the Gospel in the midst of resistance and danger. Jesus did not return in their lifetime as they had wished, but they knew that one day it would be realized. Sometimes we forget that our concept of time is different from that of the Lord.

Concerning the time of Jesus' return, we find an interesting passage in which Peter is speaking to a crowd of people after healing a crippled man who had been carried to the temple gates. After sharing the Gospel, Peter told the people that Jesus must remain in heaven until the time comes for God to restore everything as He promised long ago through his Holy prophets. This statement emphasizes that all events, including the Second Advent of Christ, will be in accordance with God's plan for humanity and the world.

Jude was the leader of the Jerusalem church and author of the epistle in his name. He wrote, "The Lord is coming with thousands upon thousands of his holy ones to judge everyone, and to convict the ungodly for the acts that they have done." He said that they are the people who speak harshly against Jesus, as well as the grumblers and faultfinders who follow their own evil desires. Jude claimed that they boast about themselves and flatter others for their own advantage. (Jude 14-16) When speaking about Jesus' return, Jude only focused upon God's judgment. He may have been reliving the actions of those with whom he had difficulty as the leader of the Jerusalem church. Jude's tone almost prevented his epistle from being included in the Scriptures. There was a concern that it was too harsh and critical. Although love should prevail, sometimes we need to identify sin.

Other disciples employed a different focus when speaking about the Second Advent. They emphasized that when Jesus returns, He expects to find elders and shepherds of God's flock who are faithful and humble in their service to others. Church leaders are reminded that God opposes the proud but gives grace to the humble. As we contemplate the return of Jesus, everyone must examine their life. Do we possess the heart and mind of our Savior? Do we see life and people through His eyes? Are we serving others in humility and love, seeking nothing in return? Like all of Jesus' teachings, understanding death and resurrection is intended to encourage us to make spiritual preparation for the next world. Regardless when we depart this earthly life, whether before or when Jesus returns, we must be prepared to stand before the Lord.

With the anticipation of Christ's appearance, the apostle John reminded fellow Christians of God's love, imploring them to be confident and unashamed at His coming. He said, "If you know that he is righteous, you know that everyone who does what is right has been born of him." John continued by saying, "Dear friends, now we are children of God, and what we will be has not yet been made known. But we know that when he appears we shall be like him, for we shall see him as he is." (I John 2:28-3:3) John wanted Christians to be worthy of God's love. He also wrote that he was not privy to all the details of our Lord's return. I have often prayed for discernment and increased knowledge. As a result, when least expected, the Lord has provided clarity for me. But I have learned that God has set boundaries on what we are to know. It is both interesting and confirming to read that even the apostle John, as close as he was to Jesus, lacked certain understandings.

— CHAPTER TWO —

# Death and Resurrection of Jesus

It is the crucifixion of Christ that has opened the door to our reconciliation with God. In accordance with the Father's will and the miraculous power of the Holy Spirit, the Son of God was born into the world. Jesus came to a humanity lost in hopelessness and sin. His Gospel was a message of salvation through repentance and faith. His incarnation was the manifestation and voice of God bringing hope to the people. His mission led to His suffering and death, and it is within this context that we find our salvation. The Lord forgives everyone, who in faith, receives Jesus into their life, acknowledging that His death was an act of love on their behalf.

It was God's will that Jesus would suffer and die a sinner's death. This is a shocking truth! But the path that led to Jesus' resurrection was His identification with the humanity that He came to save. As our Savior, God wanted Jesus to experience the agony of both the body and the soul. There is nothing that we can suffer that Jesus has not endured. This arouses His compassion for us, and within His empathy is found the grace and power to sustain us through our trials.

The crucifixion of Christ is where God's justice and love intersect. First, it was the price that was paid to save us from our sins. Jesus' death reveals the extent of our Creator's unconditional love, in that God would allow His Son to die for us. Jesus died alone and, when He took His last breath, death occurred within the Godhead. Although we cannot explain this, it is not refuted.

I sometimes think of the emotional suffering that Jesus bore, realizing what lie ahead of Him. Can you imagine ministering to others, while at the same time knowing that you will soon be tortured and crucified. Death was the greatest battle that Jesus had to face. It was far greater than the temptations in the wilderness or the dangers that He confronted as He was mindful of His own weaknesses.

During His ministry, Jesus often told His disciples that He must die and on the third day be raised from the dead. The Gospels record nine times that Jesus shared this truth with them. They did not know that it was God's will or understand the reason why it was necessary. But like a grain of wheat that dies and brings forth new life when planted in the ground, Jesus' death brought new life to the world.

Matthew tells us about a conversation between Jesus and Peter, in which Peter rebuked Jesus when He spoke about His inevitable death. Jesus in turn told Peter that it was God's will and that resisting was to do the work of Satan. This is Matthew's account of the brief exchange between Jesus and Peter:

> Jesus began to explain to his disciples that he must go to Jerusalem and suffer many things at the hands of the elders, chief priests, and teachers of the law, and that he must be killed and on the third day be raised to life. Peter took him aside and began to rebuke him. "Never, Lord,"

he said. "This shall never happen to you!" Jesus turned and said to Peter, "Out of my sight Satan! You are a stumbling block to me; you do not have in mind the things of God but the things of men." (Matthew 16:21-23)

Sometime between 740-680 B.C., Isaiah prophesied the death and resurrection of Christ:

> He was pierced for our transgressions, he was crushed for our iniquities; the punishment that brought us peace was upon him, and by his wounds we are healed. We all like sheep have gone astray, each of us has gone his own way; and the Lord has laid on him the iniquity of us all. He did not open his mouth; he was led like a lamb to the slaughter. It was the Lord's will to make him suffer and become a guilt offering, which justified many. (Isaiah 53)

Jesus experienced the suffering of humanity, knowing our temptations, trials, fears, physical and emotional pain, and spiritual battles. In dying a sinner's death, being outside of God's presence and grace, He knows the plight of the unsaved.

Matthew relates the intensity of Jesus' emotional suffering leading up to His arrest and crucifixion. With His apostles in the Garden of Gethsemane, Jesus became overwhelmed with sorrow. He fell with His face to the ground and prayed, "My Father, if it is possible, may this cup be taken from me. Yet not as I will, but as you will." (Matthew 26:36-39) When reading these words, we must remember that His emotional and physical suffering was that of humanity. We have a suffering God who died that we might live. Was the suffering and death of Jesus necessary? It was necessary because God is LOVE, and He came to save His children.

Without the death of Christ there would be no resurrection. It is the resurrection of Jesus and His promise of our victory over death that has established hope in our hearts. It is also proof of His deity and the affirmation of His teachings and promises. Without the resurrection, Jesus would simply be another martyr who died for a cause long forgotten. Let us rejoice that we have a Savior who forever lives and has opened heaven's gates to those who believe in Him.

## JESUS' DESCENT INTO HELL

The word *hell* is found at least thirty-one times in the Hebrew Bible and twenty-two times in the New Testament. As previously noted, it is commonly used to identify the place where the unrepentant go both at the time of death and after the final judgment. The Scriptures also employ other words for this location, but regardless of the terminology, it speaks to one's separation from God. As we noted, in the Apostle's Creed we read that Jesus descended into hell after His death and prior to His resurrection. This creed was finalized in 390 A.D. by Ambrose, who was the Bishop of Milan. Upon completion, it was sent to Pope Siricius in Rome. Some theologians assert that the word *hell* was not in the original creed, but that it was added at a later date.

When Jesus died, He descended into *Hades*, which is the place of departed spirits. It is believed that during His descent, He was present in the part of *Hades* where the unrighteous were. Peter states that Jesus preached to the disobedient spirits who were imprisoned during the time of Noah. He wrote, "Christ died for sins once for all, the righteous for the unrighteous, to bring you God. He was put to death in the body but made alive by the Spirit, through whom he also went and preached to the spirits in prison who disobeyed long ago when God waited patiently in the days of Noah while the ark was being built." (I Peter 3:18-20)

Although this Scripture lacks clarity and explanation, it is the basis for the belief that Jesus entered *hell*. If so, it is unknown what His message was to the lost. Some people believe that He went there to declare His victory over death, but this raises many questions. It is understandable that He would declare victory to the righteous, but there is no evidence that He made a declaration to the lost. There are scholars who contend that the imprisoned spirits include fallen angels. Peter said that God did not spare angels when they sinned, but sent them to *hell*, putting them into gloomy dungeons to be held for judgment. (II Peter 2:4) Jude wrote, "The angels who did not keep their position of authority but abandoned their own home—these he has kept in darkness, bound with everlasting chains for judgment on the Great Day." (Jude 6) Although questionable, some commentators believe that the Sons of God found in Genesis may be these fallen angels. (Genesis 6:1-4)

These passages relating to fallen angels are not supported by other Scripture, therefore, it is impossible to interpret them. We believe that Satan's fall from grace and expulsion from heaven included angels, but no details are offered. A common belief is that demonic activity includes fallen angels. If this is true, then any imprisonment of angels is limited. Imprisonment may only mean that they were cast out of heaven.

In Ephesians, Paul uses an illustration from the Scriptures which states, "When he ascended on high, he led captives in his train and gave gifts to men." (Psalm 68:18; Ephesians 4:8) This confirms what we have learned from New Testament teachings. A passage in Hebrews states that prior to Jesus' resurrection, both the unrighteous and the righteous were in *Hades* but in different locations. When Jesus entered *Hades*, He took the righteous with Him to *Paradise*. They were the faithful who had not yet received the promise. (Hebrews 11:39-40) We can conclude that Jesus did not enter *Hades* to continue atoning for our sins, for it was His death on the cross that accomplished this. On the cross He said, "It is finished!" His earthly mission was complete.

**RESURRECTION OF CHRIST**

Our hope is grounded in the resurrection of Jesus, the truths of which are found in the four Gospels and other New Testament writings. Jesus was not a martyr, for He willingly sacrificed His life and rose from the dead to show us the way to salvation. His tomb was the only one in history that was opened by heavenly messengers. Death and the grave could not hold the Son of God, nor will death hold those of faith. His resurrection in us makes our resurrection possible. When Jesus rose from the dead, He became the visible manifestation of eternal life.

Jesus did not appear to His apostles in a ghostly form, but rather as the person whom they knew. His apostles were able to see His wounds of torture and execution. The difference, however, was His ability to appear and vanish at will. This occurred when He suddenly manifested Himself to them while they were meeting behind closed doors. A similar situation involved two men that Jesus spent time with in the village of Emmaus. (Luke 24:30-31) But Jesus was the same person whose continued messages about God's kingdom brought encouragement and hope.

Because the resurrection of Jesus is at the heart of our journey of hope, I have decided to include His appearances to the apostles and others, all of which took place over a period of forty days leading up to His ascension. (Acts 1:3) This information is also found in my book titled *Christian Beliefs and Prayers*. Because these accounts are given by more than one writer, the chronology differs:

- Mary Magdalene, Mary the mother of James, and Salome, went to the tomb at dawn on the first day of the week to apply spices to Jesus' body. When they arrived, they found the sepulcher open and the body of Jesus missing. Mary Magdalene left to tell Peter and John of the situation, while the other women remained at the tomb. (John 20:1-2; Mark 16:1-4; Luke 24:1-3)

- The women who remained at the sepulcher encountered two angels who announced that Jesus had risen from the dead. They were told that Jesus would see the disciples in Galilee. (Matthew 28:5-7; Mark 16:5-7; Luke 24:4-8)

- By the time that Mary Magdalene returned to the tomb, the other women had left. As Mary was weeping, she looked into the tomb and saw two angels in white, seated where Jesus' body had been. The angels asked her why she was crying, when suddenly she saw Jesus standing there. At first, she thought that he was the gardener.

When she recognized him, he immediately told her not to hold on to him, for he had not yet returned to the Father. This indicates that Mary's relationship with Jesus was about to change, that soon he would ascend to his heavenly glory, and she would no longer see him in the flesh. After this occurred, Mary went to the apostles with the news. (Mark 16:9-11; John 20:10-18)

• Jesus appeared to Mary, the mother of James, and to Salome and Joanna, while they were on their way to the city. He repeated his message to them, that his disciples should meet him in Galilee. The women, along with others who were traveling with them, gave Jesus' message to the apostles. But the apostles did not believe that they had seen Jesus. (Matthew 28:8-12)

• Peter, and another disciple believed to have been John, ran to the tomb and found it empty. They saw the strips of linen lying there, as well as the burial cloth that had been around Jesus' head. If the body had been stolen, the wrappings would not have been removed. The position of the wrappings also made them wonder if Jesus had risen from the dead. (Luke 24:12; John 20:3-10)

• Jesus came to Peter before he appeared to the other apostles. This is reported by both Luke and Paul, but they do not provide the circumstances. (Luke 24:34; I Corinthians 15:5)

• While enroute to the village of Emmaus, which was about seven miles from Jerusalem, two believers were approached by Jesus, one of whom was named Cleopas. At first, they did not recognize him. Later in the day

Jesus ate with them, and the men suddenly realized that the one that they befriended was Jesus. Luke tells us that Jesus then disappeared from their sight. (Luke 24:13-35; Mark 16:12-13)

- Jesus appeared to the apostles when Thomas was not present. For fear of persecution, they met in a home behind locked doors. Jesus suddenly appeared in the room and showed them his hands and feet. He then said to them, "Peace be with you. As the Father has sent me, I am sending you." Jesus then breathed on them and said, "Receive the Holy Spirit." (Luke 24:36-43; John 20:19-23)

- A week later Jesus came to the apostles again, and this time Thomas was present. Thomas did not believe that the others had previously seen Jesus. He told them that he would only believe if he were able to put his finger where the nails were, and place his hand into Jesus' pierced side. Jesus told Thomas to touch his wounds and to stop doubting. After doing so, Thomas said, "My Lord and my God." Jesus then said to Thomas, "Because you have seen me you have believed; blessed are those who have not seen me and yet have believed." (John 20:24-29)

- The apostles went to a mountain where Jesus directed them to go. It was here that Jesus informed them that the Father had given him authority over heaven and earth. Then, Jesus commissioned them, saying, "Go and make disciples of all nations, baptizing them in the name of the Father and of the Son and of the Holy Spirit, and teaching them to obey everything that I have commanded you. And surely, I am with you always, to the very end of the age." (Matthew 28:16-20; Mark 16:15-18)

- Jesus appeared to his apostles by the sea of Tiberius. It was early in the morning after the apostles had a failed fishing experience the previous night. Jesus told them where to cast their net, and the results were overwhelming. Our Lord then invited them to share a breakfast of fish and bread. It was during this time that Peter was reinstated for having denied knowing Jesus after our Savior's arrest. When Peter assured Jesus of his love and commitment, Jesus commissioned him to be a shepherd of the people. (John 21:1-19)

- Paul reports that Jesus was seen by more than five hundred people at the same time. This may have been a situation when a crowd gathered where Jesus and his apostles were reported to be. When the announcement of our Lord's resurrection spread, we can be certain that people were anxious to see him, especially those who heard his teachings and witnessed his miracles. (I Corinthians 15:6)

- According to Paul, Jesus was seen by the apostle James, then by the other apostles. Paul also claims to have seen Jesus. No other information is provided. (I Corinthians 15:7)

- In the vicinity of Bethany, the apostles witnessed Jesus' ascension. When this occurred, two angels appeared to them, saying, "Men of Galilee, why do you stand here looking into the sky? This same Jesus, who has been taken from you into heaven, will come back in the same way that you have seen him go into heaven." (Mark 16:19; Luke 24:50-52; Acts 1:9-11)

- Prior to Paul accepting Jesus as his Lord and Savior, he set out on a trip to the synagogues in Damascus. He had authority from the high priest to arrest the followers of Jesus. While enroute, a light from heaven suddenly flashed around him. In the midst of the light was heard the voice of Jesus questioning Paul's intentions. (Acts 9:1-31)[2]

Jesus did not appear to the religious leaders or Roman officials, who would again seek His arrest and execution, believing that they were somehow tricked the first time. God sent Jesus to believers, who would take His message to the world.

---

[2] Henry G. Covert, *Christian Beliefs and Prayers* (La Vergne, Tennessee: Lightning Source and Ingram, 2010), 43-47.

—CHAPTER THREE—

# Eschatology

Eschatology, which is the study of the end times, involves a wide range of Scriptures from both the Hebrew Bible and the New Testament. Some theologians complicate this study by utilizing biblical passages that do not explicitly relate to our Lord's return. Speculation, combined with questionable references, only complicate what is already a difficult topic. What I offer is not an extensive study, but it does provide important insights.

Interpreting eschatological events is where scholars, lay people, and Christian communities disagree. There is no biblical subject that has caused more controversy. Interpretating Scripture on this topic includes: the tribulation, cosmic events, the Second Advent of Christ, God's judgment, the rapture of the saints, and the establishment of God's kingdom. It also involves the creation of a new heaven and earth and a perceived antichrist. The kingdom of God is two-fold, for it is within us and yet to be fulfilled when Jesus returns.

When studying eschatology, the symbolic language and veiled imagery found in the Book of Daniel and Revelation are problematic when trying to make distinctions between past biblical events, modern history, today's realities, and what is future prophecy. This is not to mention the controversy related to an antichrist, mentioned by the Apostle John. Throughout history different individuals have been identified as the antichrist. In reality, anyone whose evil seeks to block the work of the Holy Spirit is against Christ.

I interpret the tribulation as being continuous and progressive through the end of this age, intensifying prior to Jesus' return. Since recorded history, humanity has experienced persecution, natural disasters, famine, violence and wars. The torture and killing of millions of Jews and ethnic groups is a horror that is difficult to process. Most recent, is the evil slaughter in Ukraine. The violence and death attributed to hate groups and endless wars has resulted in worldwide tribulation, and according to the Scriptures, it will intensify.

In eschatology, there are three controversial schools of thought, all of which focus on the word *millennium,* which some believe speaks to a literal one thousand years when Christ will rule on earth. This word, which is found in Revelation, is at the center of the debate. It must be stated that Revelation cannot be understood literally. Although its symbolic language conveys truth, it must be framed within a broad context. (Revelation 20)

What follows are the three views:

### PREMILLENNIALISM

This understanding states that after a period of severe tribulation, Jesus will visibly return to earth, where He will set up His kingdom and rule for one thousand years. His presence and ministry will bring worldwide evangelism, resulting in countless people being saved.

After this period, the resurrection and the judgment of the unsaved will occur, followed by eternity. This is a literal view of Chapter Twenty of Revelation, however, there is no agreement as to details. Within the premillennialist understanding, there are different interpretations of the rapture, none of which have clarity.

**POSTMILLENNIALISM**

According to this view, the Second Advent of Christ will be after the *millennium,* which will be a golden age of peace and prosperity with the dominance of Christianity. This will occur through worldwide evangelism. Jesus will then establish His Kingdom on earth. This will be followed by the general resurrection, judgment, and eternity. As with the previous view, this position lacks explanation.

**AMILLENNIALISM**

This belief denies that an earthly millennium of universal righteousness and peace will either precede or follow the Second Advent. The return of Christ is at the end of the Church age, and there is no earthly millennium. The use of the word *millennium* is only symbolic, indicating a long period of time. The intermediate state of the righteous in heaven is the *millennium* alluded to in Revelation. Amillennialism spiritualizes the promises made to Israel, stating that they are fulfilled by the Church. When Jesus returns, accompanied by the saints in *Paradise,* the righteous who are alive on earth will be raptured and clothed with a new body. They will meet Jesus and His saints in the air. This will be followed by the judgment of the unrepentant and the establishment of God's eternal kingdom, which includes the new heaven and earth.

During my undergraduate studies, I enrolled in a course on Revelation. We went verse by verse through the entire book. The students, although interested in eschatology, were glad when the course was over due to the amount of energy and focus that was required. When we finished, one of the students asked the professor what his view was. He smiled and said that he was a <u>Panmillennialist</u>. When asked what he meant, the professor said that everything will pan out in the end. This was a statement acknowledging that in this life we will not have the answers.

I adhere to Amillennialism because it brings clarity and reflects what we can conclude from the Scriptures. Attempting to connect the symbolism in Revelation with passages in the Hebrew Bible is problematic. Besides, even if there is a connection, it is a puzzle that cannot be solved.

People questioned the apostles about Jesus' return. Years had gone by, and there was no indication of another appearance by Christ. Peter spoke to this issue when he wrote, "They will say, where is this coming that he promised? Ever since our fathers died, everything goes on as it has since the beginning of creation." (II Peter 3:3-4) It is understandable that the early followers of Jesus anticipated His return in their lifetime. I'm sure that the subject was often discussed among believers, including the apostles. Even today there have been dates given by certain groups, sometimes with ulterior motives.

Peter told fellow Christians that "with the Lord a day is

like a thousand years and a thousand years like a day. The Lord is not slow about his promises, as some understand slowness. He is patient toward us, not wanting anyone to perish, but everyone to come to repentance." (II Peter 3:8-9) Peter wanted inquisitors to know that God's patience means salvation for people who otherwise would not be saved. He seems to be implying that Jesus' delay is rooted in God's love. Jesus told His apostles that only the Father knew when His return would occur. He said, "No one knows about that day or hour, not even the angels in heaven, nor the Son, but only the Father." As it was in the days of Noah and the flood, the time will be decided by the Father. (Mark 13:32-33)

God's eternal kingdom will be realized after the destruction of this planet. This truth is revealed in both the Hebrew Bible and the New Testament. In the Hebrew Scriptures, the prophets Isaiah and Malachi wrote about the earth's destruction and how God will create a new heaven and earth. (Isaiah 66:22; Malachi 4) Peter emphasized this cosmic event, saying, "The day of the Lord will come like a thief in the night. The heavens will disappear with a roar, the elements will be destroyed by fire, and the earth and everything in it will be laid bare." (II Peter 3:10) The words of the Hebrew prophets, the apostles, and Jesus, clearly state that there will be a new creation for God's people. (Revelation 21:1-8)

I have intentionally not touched upon other questionable areas relating to the end times. Each subject would require another book, and in the end we would find ourselves back at the beginning. I enjoy a challenge, but I have learned when to conclude a study.

— CHAPTER FOUR —

# The Judgment

The Scriptures provide many truths concerning God's judgment. The author of Hebrews tells us that we are "destined to die once, and after that to face judgment." (Hebrews 9:27) We also know that the Father has entrusted the judgment of humanity to Christ in order that He will be honored just as the Father is honored. (John 5:22-23) In both the Hebrew Bible and the New Testament we learn that the Lord will reward everyone according to what he has done. (Psalm 62:12; Revelation 22:12-13) We must not understand this within the context of works righteousness, meaning that we are judged simply on the number of good deeds that we do. Instead, it is a matter of faith and the heart. If we love the Lord and walk in the Spirit, our deeds will emanate from a pure heart. As the saying goes, "Whitewashing the pump doesn't make the water pure." What we see on the outside doesn't always reflect the reality inside. God's displeasure with Cain's offering was the attitude of his heart.

God's judgment will examine every aspect of our lives. In Hebrews we read, "Nothing in all creation is hidden from God's sight. Everything is uncovered and laid bare before the eyes of him to whom we must give account." (Hebrews 4:13) Paul said that

God will judge men's secrets. (Romans 2:16) In his book *Do We Know Jesus?* Adolf Schlatter wrote, "God's judgment will be based on what we hide. A human judge must restrict himself to what can be arrived at on the basis of human testimony. Therefore, human judgment never has the absolute last word. In light of the divine presence, however, there is no longer anything in the dark."[3]

We sometimes become discouraged when we see deceptive and evil people doing well in life, often at the expense of others. But we must remember that at the end of this brief life everyone will stand before the Lord.

The traditional belief is that there will be one general judgment, but some students of Scripture point to multiple judgments. There are biblical passages that suggest this, but they appear to relate to different aspects of the same judgment. Believers will stand before the throne of Christ, but it will not be a judgment that condemns them. Instead, it will be a review of their lives in which lessons will be learned. The sins of the faithful have been forgiven. This is repeatedly confirmed in the teachings of Jesus and throughout the New Testament.

The apostle John was given a vision in which he saw the judgment of the unsaved:

> Then I saw a great white throne and him who was seated on it. Earth and sky fled from his presence, and there was no place for them. And I saw the dead, great and small, standing before the throne, and books were opened. Another book was opened, which is the Book of

---

[3] Adolf Schlatter, *Do We Know Jesus?* (Grand Rapids, Michigan: Kregel Publications, 2005), 310.

Life. The dead were judged according to what they had done as recorded in the book. The sea gave us the dead that were in it, and death and Hades gave up the dead that were in them, and each person was judged according to what he had done. Then death and Hades were thrown into the lake of fire. The lake of fire is the second death. If anyone's name was not found in the Book of Life, he was thrown into the lake of fire. (Revelation 20:11-15)

According to John's vision, those who are not found in the Book of Life will be eternally separated from God. The judgment will include fallen angels who abandoned their positions of authority. They have been kept in darkness and will be held accountable for their sins against God and humanity.

Our humility and how we treat others will also impact God's judgement. "The Beatitudes" are an example of God's mercy toward the downtrodden and the outcasts of society. On a Galilean hillside overlooking Capernaum, Jesus taught the people, saying:

> Blessed are the poor in spirit, for theirs is the kingdom of heaven.
> Blessed are those who mourn, for they will be comforted.
> Blessed are the meek, for they will inherit the earth.
> Blessed are those who hunger and thirst for righteousness, for they will be filled.
> Blessed are the merciful, for they will be shown mercy.
> Blessed are the pure in heart, for they shall see God.

> Blessed are the peacemakers, for they will be called sons of God.
>
> Blessed are those who are persecuted because of righteousness, for theirs is the kingdom of heaven.
>
> Blessed are you, when people insult you, and falsely say all kinds of evil against you because of me.
>
> Rejoice and be glad, because great is your reward in heaven, for in the same way they persecuted the prophets who were before you. (Matthew 5:1-12)

James spoke about the needy when he wrote, "Has not God chosen those who are poor in the eyes of the world to be rich in faith and to inherit the kingdom he promised to those who love him?" (James 2:5) He continued by stressing that the wealthy who live only for themselves will suffer the consequences. In strong words he said, "Your wealth has rotted, and moths have eaten your clothes. Your gold and silver are corroded. Their corrosion will testify against you and eat your flesh like fire." (James 5:2-3) Jesus told His disciples that it is easier for a camel to go through the eye of a needle than for a rich man to enter the kingdom of God. (Matthew 19:23-24)

Again, it is not a matter of the rich versus the poor, but rather those who trust in their wealth to the exclusion of God and others. Jesus knew that many people place their trust in money rather than in God. It is interesting that our currency is printed with the words, *In God We Trust*. This is a reminder that we are not to trust in our wealth.

The judgment will also involve our willingness to forgive others. Jesus tells us to forgive all people, including those whom we believe are enemies. In fact, our forgiveness is rooted in this truth. We must forgive in order for God to forgive us. Even when we pray, God will not hear us if we are holding anything against another person. Forgiving others is a response that emanates from the inner life. In other words, it is a matter of the heart. Mercy, love, and forgiveness are intertwined, for you cannot have one without the other. In the "Beatitudes" Jesus said, "Blessed are the merciful, for they shall be shown mercy." Although this is a spiritual truth, it is also a truth that impacts our daily life.

Paul tells us that without love our accomplishments and actions are meaningless. He included faith in this teaching, for what good is faith if our heart lacks love? Paul wrote the Corinthians that faith, hope, and love, are essential to our Christian life, with the greatest being love. (I Corinthians 13) Kierkegaard said, "To imitate Christ is to imitate love, and that love includes building up love in others." This means that loving others implants love in them.[4] To love all people we must have the love of Christ in us. This speaks to a changed heart that comes through faith and prayer.

Jesus gave His last breath for all sinners, and this presents a question. How can we hate those for whom Jesus gave His life? While we may hate a person's sin, we must never hate the person. The life and death of Christ exemplifies this truth. But is this possible, especially in certain situations? It may be a process, but it is possible through earnest prayer for oneself and the person causing us pain. How can we continue to hate someone for whom we pray?

---

[4] Sylvia Walsh, *Kierkegaard and Religion* (United Kingdom and New York: Cambridge University Press, 2018), 162.

Prison ministry challenged my spiritual life in many ways. I often prayed for the heart of Christ, realizing how difficult it was to love certain offenders. How could I minister to these men without the love of Christ in me? Without being able to love unconditionally, my position was meaningless. A prison chaplain is being a pastor to some of society's most troubled and violent individuals. I often prayed for God's anointing love, enabling me to see their pain instead of their crime and personality.

We live in a world of false gods and deception, and the power of these forces lead people away from God and into self-destruction. Kierkegaard spoke about this in his writings. He said that looking to the senses and worldly things to find meaning and fulfillment results in despair. He refers to such people as "The Society of the Dead." These are people who live with illusions to the very end. They believe that their despair results from not being able to fill the voids in their life. But the truth is that the despair is within them as they try to live without God.[5]

According to Kierkegaard, "The world is a place of darkness and untruthful corruption. Life without God is like walking through a thick forest. We cannot discern a clear path ahead without a guide." Rather than being enmeshed in the world, we must tend to the inner life that feeds the soul. Whether it is in prison or a community parish, pastors are charged with leading people away from a worldly lifestyle that thwarts the movement of the Holy Spirit.[6]

---

[5]  Ibid., 12-13, 24-25, 56-58.

[6]  Clare Carlisle, *Philosopher of the Heart: The Restless Life of Soren Kierkegaard* (New York: Farrar, Straus, and Giroux, 2019), 170, 188.

Realizing our need for God's grace humbles us and leaves no room for pride and personal merit. Kierkegaard emphasized that everything is from God. His favorite Scripture verse is from James 1:17, which states, "Every good and perfect gift is from above, coming down from the Father of the heavenly lights, who does not change like shifting shadows."[7] John Wesley said that everything we have is a gift from God and must be used for His glory through the life that we live.

Kierkegaard taught that "selfishness" is the key obstacle between God and people. It is through selfishness that the world has power over us. Selfishness also prevents equality, for we can possess what others cannot have, but Kierkegaard admitted that giving up selfishness is a continuous spiritual battle. The riches that we have stored up for ourselves, to the exclusion of others, will follow us to the grave and determine our eternal destiny. It is only by dying to self that we can die to the world and receive the gifts of the Spirit.[8]

All preaching and Church education must emphasize mercy. Unlike the world, Jesus left His robes of glory to become a servant to all people. He came to get involved with the sick and dying, giving hope to the outcasts and those living on the fringes of society. There was nothing in His nature that was self-serving. These are important truths to ponder when contemplating God's judgment.

Jesus repeatedly emphasized that God is love, and when we love others, we experience the presence of divine love within us.

---

[7]   Ibid., 149, 226.

[8]   Sylvia Walsh, *Kierkegaard and Religion* (United Kingdom and New York: Cambridge University Press, 2018), 134.

Paul tells us that in Christ we become new creatures, that the self-centered life becomes God-centered. It is a sacrificial life that flows from a changed heart. Love is not a once in a while response depending upon conditions and circumstances, but rather a natural response to humanity and the world around us. It is who we have become as we possess the heart and mind of Jesus. When we die, the only thing that we can take with us is the love that we have given away.

The true test of love is how we respond to others, including those outside of our comfort zone. Jesus tells us to do good to those who hate and mistreat us. He told His apostles, "If you only love those who love you, what credit is that to you? Even sinners love those who love them. Be merciful, just as your heavenly Father is merciful." (Luke 6:27-36) Jesus' commands to the apostles centered on God's love, when He said:

> As the Father has loved me, so have I loved you. Now remain in my love. If you obey my commands, you will remain in my love, just as I have obeyed my Father's commands and remain in his love. I have told you this so that my joy may be in you and that your joy may be complete. My command is this: Love each other as I have loved you. Greater love has no one than this, that one lay down his life for his friends. You are my friends, if you do what I command. (John 15:9-14)

These words were realized when Jesus was arrested and led to Golgotha to be crucified. In the midst of the excruciating pain of execution His love continued to reach out to others, including His mother and John who were present. Then, we hear

Jesus' words asking His Father to forgive those who had sealed His death, because they did not know the gravity of what they were doing. To speak about love is one thing, but to see the suffering of love pierces the heart. We have a choice to either live in love or to live in anger and hate. Recently, my wife and I were walking the streets of a small country town when I noticed these words on a shop window, *I have decided on love. Hate is too much of a burden to bear.* What an insightful and powerful statement!

We must develop our inner life, and the process begins when we surrender our will to God, allowing the Holy Spirit to guide us on our journey. Our judgment will be focused on the inner life and what we have done for the glory of God. It is the inner life that speaks to the love and mercy that results in the self-denial revealed in Christ. Kierkegaard wrote, "Christ not only practiced self-denial by taking the form of a lowly servant, walking about defenseless, and surrendering all power; he was *self-denial* itself, requiring of his disciples the very same conditions of lowliness and contempt that he endured."[9]

In her book titled *Kierkegaard and Religion*, Sylvia Walsh wrote, "The religiosity of our age reflects the 'feel good,' undemanding spirituality so severely criticized by Kierkegaard in his time." She continued by saying that rather than being concerned about the inner life, people gravitate toward self-interest and self-aggrandizement in an attempt to meet their needs. "Our prototypes for self-development are sports heroes, entertainment stars, gun-toting Rambos, and corporate CEOs, not Jesus of Nazareth."

---

[9] Ibid., 131, 135-136.

Although we are sympathetic toward others during times of crisis, it is often short-lived.[10]

The following teaching of Jesus was recalled by Matthew. It speaks to our mercy toward others and how it will impact God's judgment. Jesus shared these words after telling His disciples that He will separate the saints from the unrighteous when He returns:

> Then the King will say to those on his right, "Come, you who are blessed by my Father, take your inheritance, the kingdom prepared for you since the creation of the world. For I was hungry, and you gave me something to eat. I was thirsty, and you gave me something to drink. I was a stranger, and you invited me in. I needed clothes, and you clothed me. I was sick, and you looked after me. I was in prison, and you came to visit me." Then the righteous will answer him, "Lord, when did we see you hungry and feed you, or thirsty and give you something to drink? When did we see you a stranger and invite you in, or needing clothes and clothe you? When did we see you sick or in prison and go to visit you?" The King will reply, "I tell you the truth, whatever you did for one of the least of these brothers of mine, you did for me." Then he will say to those on his left, "Depart from me, you who are cursed, into the eternal fire prepared for the devil and his angels." (Matthew 25:31-41)

I cannot imagine anyone not being moved by our Lord's words in this passage. In a heart-searching way, Jesus probes our

---

[10] Ibid., 178-179.

inner life. His words force us to see who we are and who we should prayerfully strive to be. Yes, we are the keepers of our brothers and sisters, and we will be judged accordingly. While history reveals intense evil, there have always been servants of God who have dedicated their life to the needs of others. What would the world be like without these individuals and the volunteer organizations, such as doctors without borders and free medical clinics? I shrink when thinking about such people. In the church that I pastored after leaving the prison, there were elderly folks who exemplified humility and service to God and others. My wife and I frequently recall the many blessings of those years.

In the passage that we just read, Jesus tells us that whatever we do for others, we are also doing it for Him. In reality, His ministry is ours, and our ministry is His. We are an extension of Christ in the world for which He died. I have often told people that I felt more like a pastor when ministering to the needs of people than with any other aspect of church life. The ministry of presence is living the Gospel message. It is putting the teachings of Christ into action. After all, love isn't love until you give it away.

When speaking about love, diversity comes to my mind. The kingdom of God will certainly be diverse, for it will include people from all races and nations. Knowing this should move us to examine our attitudes toward those from other cultures and nationalities. All the laws in the world cannot change the human heart. Recently, I was teaching a course on prison ministry at a church near my residence. Most of those in attendance were educated and committed church members. At one point I mentioned the diversity of my prison congregation, and to my surprise I heard someone say, "What good is diversity?" I was shocked! Teachers hear some interesting responses, but this was something that I never expected in a church environment. Hopefully, I responded in love.

Diversity is of God! It is diversity that enables us to understand the world through the cultures, traditions, and beliefs of others. Most of the world's population are people of color, however, I question how many people consider this when they contemplate Christianity. In the eyes of God, there is one humanity. The prejudices harbored within the Church must be topics that are addressed in the preaching and educational programs of faith communities. Only the pure in heart will enter God's kingdom.

Those who are prejudiced, self-absorbed, and insensitive to the cries of humanity fail to comprehend the meaning and purpose of life. Although there are limitations when helping people, there is always a way to show kindness. Sometimes it may simply be a gentle smile or being a compassionate listener. I learned this in the prison system where I often had to refuse an inmate request. But whatever I could not do for an inmate I tried to replace it with something that was possible.

The "Parable of Lazarus and the Rich Man" exemplifies those who are oblivious to another person's needs and suffering. What is shocking is the rich man's response when he died. Even when he found himself outside of God's grace, he still didn't get it. This is the story of so many people who will face the judgment, failing to see the error of their ways. We are saved by faith and grace, but faith is empty without mercy and love.

Sometimes life brings us to a place when we must make a decision that will lead us down a precarious path. It may even be standing up against evil that takes human life. Such was the case with Dietrich Bonhoeffer. As a scholar and Lutheran pastor who came from a prestigious German family, Bonhoeffer was assured of an excellent future. But as Nazi atrocities became known, he refused to take the path of other ministers who aligned themselves with Adolf Hitler. He broadcasted anti-Nazi messages, dangerously worked behind the scenes to obtain intelligence, and he started his own seminary for students who stood firm with him. After much prayer and struggle, he became involved in the plot to kill Hitler. The struggle involved his beliefs regarding the taking of life.

But Bonhoeffer reached a point of no return. He is quoted as saying, "Silence in the face of evil is evil itself. God will not hold us guiltless. Not to speak is to speak. Not to act is to act." He was eventually imprisoned by the Gestapo, but he was offered release if he recanted his statements and supported the Third Reich. He refused, and on April 9, 1945, at the age of thirty-nine, he was executed by hanging at the Flossenburg Concentration Camp in Bavaria, Germany. It was just a few weeks before the end of the war. As the noose was placed around his neck, he said, "This is the end for me, the beginning of life." Bonhoeffer's brother and two of his brother-in-laws were also executed.

> The prison doctor at Flossenburg gave this account: Through the half-open door in one room of the huts I saw Pastor Bonhoeffer, before taking off his prison garb, kneeling on the floor fervently praying to God. I was most deeply moved by the way this lovable man prayed, so devout and so certain that God heard his prayer. At

the place of execution, he again said a short prayer and then climbed the steps to the gallows, brave and composed. His death ensued after a few seconds. In the almost fifty-five years that I worked as a doctor, I have hardly seen a man die so entirely submissive to the will of God.[11]

Dietrich Bonhoeffer gave his life to the teachings and promises of Jesus, knowing that his death was merely a transition from this world to God's realm. Like the apostle Paul, there remained work for him to do, but in faith he submitted to God's will. Although his life was brief, it was one that continues to be a witness of what it means to be a disciple of Jesus Christ.

I have been a student of Bonhoeffer's writings for many years. His book *The Cost of Discipleship* is required reading in seminaries all over the world, primarily because of its deep theological thought and his beliefs concerning discipleship. During the Third Reich when pastors were bending to Nazi Germany, Bonhoeffer continuously asked fellow Christians, "Who is Christ for us today? Has the Gospel message changed?" This is a question that everyone needs to ponder.

While Bonhoeffer was suffering in his prison cell, he was continuously ministering to other inmates, often speaking to them through solid walls. In the midst of his own pain and, with the knowledge that he would soon be executed, his compassion and mercy was evident during his entire incarceration. We may not be faced with the decisions that Bonhoeffer had to make, but

---

[11] Eric Metaxas, *Bonhoeffer Abridged: Pastor, Martyr, Prophet, Spy* (Nashville, Tennessee: Nelson Books, 2014), 209.

we must examine our inner life and pray for the strength and love to help those in need. There is no greater life than being a disciple of forgiveness and love. Like the "Good Samaritan" who never thought that he would be attending to an enemy's needs, we never know who the Lord will send to us. We tend to highlight individuals who are known to us, but there are everyday people who reach out to others as they journey through life. Although we must be cautious in terms of our interactions, there are certainly situations in which we can show mercy.

Sometime between 605-536 B.C., the prophet Daniel foretold the end times, when there would be deep distress, the resurrection, and God's judgment. He said, "At that time Michael, the great prince who protects your people, will arise. There will be a time of distress such as has not happened from the beginning of nations until then. But at that time your people—everyone whose name is found written in the book—will be delivered." (Daniel 12:1) John the Baptist told the people that "Whoever believes in the Son has eternal life, but whoever rejects the Son will not see life, for God's wrath remains on him." (John 3:36)

According to Paul, everyone will appear before the Lord, but the righteous are in God's favor. There are two references relating to this, both of which were written by Paul. He told the Christians in Rome that we shall all stand before God's judgment seat and confess our sins. Also, to the Church in Corinth he wrote, "We must all appear before the judgment seat of Christ, that each one may receive what is due him for the things done while in the body, whether good or bad." (Romans 14:11; II Corinthians 5:10)

Paul's understanding is somewhat ambiguous, but one can assume that the reward given to each will either be eternal life in God's kingdom or eternal punishment. It is doubtful that separate rewards will be given for specific things. When referring to judgment and punishment, the Scriptures employ words such as: *the second death, outer darkness, hell, lake of fire, and the fiery furnace.* The purpose of these words is to convey the pain experienced by those who will enter eternity without God.

In the "Parable of the Dragnet" Jesus provides powerful imagery of the judgment:

> The kingdom of heaven is like a net that was let down into the lake and caught all kinds of fish. When it was full, the fishermen pulled it up on the shore. Then they sat down and collected the good fish in baskets, but threw the bad away. This is how it will be at the end of the age. The angels will come and separate the wicked from the righteous and throw them into the fiery furnace, where there will be weeping and gnashing of teeth. (Matthew 13:47-52)

Fishing was a main source of livelihood and diet during the time of Christ, and Jesus used the imagery of commercial fishing to explain God's judgment, when the righteous will be separated from the unrepentant. The certainty of the judgment speaks to our accountability before God and humanity. We are reminded that our life must be a gift for others, and our responsibility is universal.

While this teaching is a warning, it is also a message of comfort and hope for those who come to the Lord. Knowing that we are accountable before God should lead us, in humility and faith, to seek forgiveness and grace while there is time. This is the central truth of the parable. In His love, Jesus repeatedly warns us about the realities of life and death, and this parable is another clear and graphic example.

One day the net will be cast, and the angels will go forth to separate humanity. It is tragic to think that so many people will face their eternal destiny having chosen to live without God. Jesus told His disciples that they must work while there is daylight. This reveals God's love and the urgency of the Gospel message. God, in His mercy, relentlessly tries to save us from self-destruction and the wrath that is to come, but His pleas so often fall upon deaf ears. As our heavenly parent, the Lord calls us into His safety and eternal rest. As parents, all we can do is warn our children about life's dangers, but the decisions will be made by them. We can only hope and pray that they choose the correct path.

The apostle John heard the voice of Jesus say, "Behold, I am coming soon. My reward is with me, and I will give to everyone according to what he has done. I am the Alpha and the Omega, the First and the Last, the beginning and the End. Blessed are those who wash their robes, that they may have the right to the tree of life, and may go through the gates into the city." (Revelation 22:12-14)

— CHAPTER FIVE —

## Eternity with the Lord

*Think of stepping on shore and finding it heaven.*
*Of taking hold of a hand and finding it God's hand*
*Of breathing new air and finding it celestial air.*
*Of feeling invigorated and finding it immortality.*
*Of passing from storm to tempest to an unbroken calm.*
*Of waking up and finding it heaven.*

(unknown writer—excerpt attributed
to composer Don Wyrtzen)

Jesus tells us that in His Father's house there are many mansions or rooms, and that He is preparing a place for us. (John 14:2-6) The Greek word for *mansion* is defined as a special place of abode. When thinking about Jesus' words, I expand its meaning to include all of God's creation, for the entire created order belongs to God to be used for His purposes and glory. Jesus does not clarify whether He is referring to *Paradise*, which is an intermediate state, or if He is speaking about where we will spend eternity at the end of the age. But regardless of time and location, it is where we experience the glory of our Creator.

In the prophecies of Israel there arose the belief that God would create a new heaven and earth, or that what presently exists would be renewed by an act of God. But who could imagine such a cosmic event? However, the Scriptures confirm that the current form and state of nature is not the final place that God has in mind for us. The belief of a new created world is based upon both the Hebrew Bible and New Testament teachings. The present world is tainted and broken by sin, and it will be replaced.

Around 690 B.C., the prophet Isaiah told the Jewish nations that the heavens will vanish like smoke, and the earth will wear out like a garment. (Isaiah 51:6; Matthew 5:18, 24:35) Isaiah continued his prophecy when he said, "Behold, I will create new heavens and a new earth. The former things will not be remembered, nor will they come to mind. The new heavens and the new earth that I will make will endure before me, so will your name and descendants endure." (Isaiah 65:17, 66:22)

Paul said, "No eye has seen, nor ear has heard, no mind has conceived what God has prepared for those who love him." (I Corinthians 2:9) In a vision, John saw a new heaven and earth, revealing God's promise to make all things new:

> I saw the holy city, the new Jerusalem, coming down out of heaven prepared as a bride beautifully dressed for her husband. And I heard a loud voice from the throne, saying, "Now the dwelling of God is with men, and he will live with them and be their God. He will wipe away every tear from their eyes. There will be no more death, or mourning or crying or pain, for the old order of things has passed away." He who was seated on the throne said, "I am making everything new!" Then he said, "Write this down, for these words are trustworthy and true." He said

to me, "It is done. I am the Alpha and the Omega, the Beginning and the End. To him who is thirsty I will give to drink without cost from the spring of the water of life. He who overcomes will inherit all this, and I will be his God, and he will be my son. But the cowardly, the unbelieving, the vile, the murderers, the sexually immoral, those who practice magic arts, the idolaters, and all the liars—their place will be in the fiery lake of burning sulfur. This is the second death." (Revelation 21:1-8)

The Jews believed that Jerusalem, with its divinely appointed Temple, was the holiest place on earth. In particular, was the inner sanctuary at the west end of the Temple where the Holy of Holies was located. This room enshrined the Ark of the Covenant that contained the Ten Commandments given to Moses on Mount Sinai, Aaron's rod which had divine power, and a gold pot filled with the manna that sustained the Israelites during their forty years in the wilderness.

The Holy of Holies was a symbol of Israel's special relationship with God. It was a dark room, whose only light came from the glow of God's glory. According to Jewish tradition, this holy place was considered the spiritual junction between heaven and earth. Only the high priest was permitted within this hallowed sanctuary. Once a year, on the Day of Atonement, the high priest would enter the Holy of Holies to atone for his sins and those of the people. With the spiritual significance given to the Temple and Holy of Holies, it is understandable why the city of Jerusalem was and continues to be considered the holiest place on earth by the Jews. This is where God chose to manifest himself and be worshiped.

These understandings are important because they speak to John's vision and the ushering in of God's kingdom. John was given a revelation that the Israelites would receive with the hope of God's ultimate and final deliverance of the people. There is truth in this allegory for people of every age, which certainly includes the Church. It is a picture of God's eternal reward for the righteous, those who have overcome the challenges and struggles of life through their unwavering faith. For Christians, it is the new heaven and earth.

Another vision given to John provides additional insights into the city that awaits us. It is an affirmation that the presence of the Lord will eternally reside with us.

> Then the angel showed me the river of the water of life, as clear as crystal, flowing from the throne of God and the Lamb, down the middle of the great street of the city. On each side of the river stood the tree of life, bearing twelve crops of fruit, yielding its fruit every month. And the leaves of the tree are for the healing of the nations. No longer will there be any curse. The throne of God and the Lamb will be in the city, and his servants will serve him. They will see his face, and his name will be on their foreheads. There will be no night. They will not need the the light of a lamp or the light of the sun, for the Lord will give them light. And they will reign for ever and ever. (Revelation 22:1-5)

These verses reveal important truths about our eternal future. The descriptive phrases indicate fullness of life and continuous blessings. The early Jews looked forward to a new Jerusalem that would be free of oppression and fear. What was lost in Eden's paradise because of sin will be restored. Paul reminds us that the faithful are heirs of God's restoring glory. Our inheritance will remove the veil and enable us to see and learn unimaginable truths that Paul could only glimpse when God permitted him to see *Paradise*. Concerning death, Socrates said, "You need to die in order to live. Why resist death? You will finally get all the answers to everything that you wanted to know." I'm reminded of the words to a country song that says *"We all want to get to heaven, but we don't want to die to get there."* I'm sure that many people would prefer another way to make the trip.

I experienced the anxiety of many individuals who had terminal illnesses. Regardless of one's faith, this is a natural response to an overwhelming situation. It is a time when thoughts and emotions need to be processed. It is difficult to think that we are leaving the only world that we know, people who we love, and everything that holds meaning for us. There is even anxiety when we realize that no words can comfort us. But as death approaches, many people report feeling an unexplained peace and comfort.

Years ago, I was in a violent motorcycle accident. It was on a beautiful fall afternoon. I had just finished preaching at two churches, and I was looking forward to getting on my Harley for a ride. At the time, my wife was out of town visiting a close friend. Within fifteen minutes after leaving my home, a truck turned in front of me. Unable to avoid the collision, I struck the truck while traveling 55 miles an hour. After being ejected from the motorcycle, I first landed on the highway and was nearly run over by oncoming traffic. I then rolled into a ditch along the highway, where I was losing consciousness. As pain was radiating through my body, I was experiencing anxiety thinking about my wife's response when she learned of the accident. Fortunately, after nine months of physical therapy and two surgeries, I regained my health.

The postscript to this incident is what I was thinking and feeling, believing that I was close to death. Thoughts about my wife and family immediately surfaced. I was concerned about their feelings and welfare. I wondered if I would be able to see and speak with them one more time. When nearing death, our loved ones are our first concern. But as I was being attended by ambulance personnel and others at the scene, I began to experience a strong sense of peace that was overcoming my pain. I am certain that it was divinely given to assure me that I was not alone.

## THOUGHTS AND QUESTIONS ABOUT HEAVEN

The Scriptures provide a sketch about the end times, but there are many questions relating to our heavenly home:

> Considering the many languages in the world, how will we communicate?
> What about nutrition?
> In what way will the learning process continue?
> Will our sleeping habits be similar to those in the present?
> Will we still have free will. If so, to what extent?
> Will it be possible to commit sin?
> What about aging? Will everyone age, or will it terminate at a certain point?
> Are there animals in God's kingdom?
> Will we travel or stay in one location? What about interplanetary travel?

Will the weather remain constant or change as it does on earth?
Whom will we meet and spend time with?
Will we see family, friends, and saints from the past?
Will we interact with beings from other locations in the universe?
Will transportation be necessary?
What types of activities will there be?
What about lodging?
Will we maintain our present names?
Will we be engaged in some type of work?
Will our relationships include heavenly beings, such as angels?
Will there be a consciousness of time?
Will there be a remembrance of our past earthly life?

These are only some of the many questions that leave us without answers. There is a time for everything in accordance with God's perfect wisdom, and eventually the answers will come.

Louis of Blois, a Belgium Benedictine Abbot, who died in 1566, shared his personal thoughts with a writing titled *Bathed in the Essence of God*:

> When through love, the soul goes beyond all
> the images of the mind, and is taken out of itself,
> it flows into God. Then is God its peace and fullness.
> It loses itself in the Godhead; but to lose itself
> is rather to find itself. The soul is, at it were all God-
> colored, because its essence is bathed in the essence of God.

In life, we make choices and set priorities, both of which influence the path that we will travel. Most of our time is given to secular activities, which we determine to be important. In the "Parables of the Hidden Treasure and the Pearl of Great Price," Jesus speaks to choices in terms of what is temporary and that which is eternal:

> The kingdom of heaven is like a treasure hidden in a field. When a man found it, he hid it again, and then in his joy went and sold all that he had and bought the field. Again, the kingdom of heaven is like a merchant looking for fine pearls. When he found one of great value, he went away and sold everything he had and bought it. (Matthew 13:44-46)

If we know that nothing is more important than our relationship with God, then why is it so difficult to change our priorities? To contemplate our death and how our present life influences eternity is a topic that people resist. We find it easier to focus on this world and talk about lighthearted things. I once asked a teenage Sunday school class what they would give to live forever in a perfect environment. I described a place of love that met all of their needs. Without exception, each one agreed that they would give up everything, even their prized possessions. What astonished me were their responses when I told them that this place was God's eternal kingdom. Their thoughts were completely focused upon the temporary things of this world. Regardless of age, many people do not think about life beyond the present.

When the man found the treasure in the field, what did he do? With joy, he sold all that he had and purchased the field. Further, to be certain that the treasure would not be taken from him, he hid it again. This parable addresses our priorities and what is most valuable to us. Jesus reminds us that the cost of discipleship is a surrendered life. (Matthew 10:32-39)

In the second parable, the merchant searched for a pearl of great value. Willing to pay any price, the man sold everything he had to possess the costly pearl, knowing that it was priceless and could not be duplicated. Jesus tells us that the man searched for the pearl, and this is an important point. In other words, he spent his time and energy to find what he knew was more valuable than anything that he owned. We must ask ourselves what we are willing to give for the priceless gift of salvation.

Jesus once spoke to a Samaritan woman who was drawing water from Jacob's well. He told her that if she knew whom she was talking to, that she would ask Him for living water. He was obviously testing her. She responded by asking Jesus where she could get this water. Her thoughts were unquestionably grounded in this life.

Regarding priorities, I am reminded of a story that Luke tells us:

> As Jesus and his disciples were on their way, he came to a village where a woman named Martha opened her home to him. She had a sister called Mary, who sat at the Lord's feet listening to what he said. But Martha was distracted by all the preparations that had to be made. She came to Jesus and asked, "Lord, don't you care that

my sister has left me to do the work by myself? Tell her to help me!" "Martha, Martha," the Lord answered, "you are worried and upset about many things, but only one thing is needed. Mary has chosen what is better, and it will not be taken away from her." (Luke 10:38-42)

After preaching a sermon on this text, a woman approached me as she was leaving church. She was very upset, feeling that Jesus was insensitive to the fact that Martha needed help, especially since the meal was for Him. Even after explaining the point of the message, she was still frustrated. Her last words were, "Women need help in the kitchen." Later, I wondered what took place in her home around mealtime.

Life is full of choices, and they make a difference on our earthly journey. In fact, one decision can forever change our lives. Although I was in the Navy during a dangerous time, I almost made the choice to reenlist. How would this have impacted my life? I also thought about my law enforcement career in the same way, having left before I was entitled to a pension. I have fond memories of both careers, but I had to make choices. In the end, I chose to respond to what I sensed was the Lord's calling into the ministry, even though I knew that it would be an arduous road with no guarantees. The one choice that we all must make, however, is whether we will embark upon the journey that leads to God.

— CHAPTER SIX —

# The Spirit World

## SATAN AND DEMONS

The apostle Paul wrote, "We do not wrestle against flesh and blood, but against the principalities, against the powers, against the rulers of darkness of this age, against the hosts of wickedness in the heavenly places." (Ephesians 6:10-18)

The reality of Satan is taught in seven books of the Hebrew Bible and by every New Testament writer. Jesus continually acknowledged the existence and power of Satan and what his mission is in the world. The prophet Ezekiel wrote about Satan's fall from grace:

> You were anointed as a guardian cherub, for so I ordained you. You were on the holy mount of God; you walked among the fiery stones. You were blameless in your ways from the day you were created, till wickedness was found in you. Through your widespread trade you were filled with violence, and you sinned. So, I drove you in disgrace from the mount of God, and I expelled you, O guardian cherub, from among the fiery stones. Your heart became proud on account of your beauty, and you corrupted your wisdom because of your splendor. So, I threw you to earth; I made a spectacle of you before

kings. By your many sins and dishonest trade you have desecrated your sanctuaries. (Ezekiel 28:14-18)

In the New Testament, we learn of a war in heaven in which Satan and his angels lost their privileged positions:

> And there was a war in heaven. Michael and his angels fought against the dragon, and the dragon and his angels fought back. But he was not strong enough, and they lost their place in heaven. The great dragon was hurled down—that ancient serpent called the devil or Satan, who leads the world astray. He was hurled to the earth, and his angels with him. (Revelation 12:7-9)

Satan is given ten different names and titles in the New Testament, including "the god of this age." He is represented as the serpent, dragon, and angel of light. In his pride, he wanted to possess heaven and earth. His earthly mission has always been to thwart the redemptive work of Christ and to deceive the nations. (Matthew 2:16, 16:23; John 8:44, 13:27; Rev. 20:3) In preparation for His ministry, Jesus was led by the Spirit into the desert to be tempted by the devil. Satan tempted Christ by focusing upon human weakness, faith, pride, and power. In each instance Jesus defended Himself with God's Word. Satan finally retreated, but the battle was far from over.

The temptation of Christ holds many truths for us. First, it emphasizes that no one is exempt from temptation. If Satan tempted the Son of God, we can be assured that we will always be a target of his evil. Secondly, the weapons that the devil used upon Jesus are the same weapons that he employs with us. So many people have been destroyed by pride, power, greed, and the lack of faith. We find these same temptations in the Garden of Eden. Lastly, Jesus stood on God's Word, which caused Satan to flee. The Word of God is our defense, but how many people have internalized God's Word and the promises of Jesus? Like soldiers preparing their weapons for war, we must always be prepared to stand firm against evil. Sometimes we forget that, although life has wonderful experiences, we are still in the middle of spiritual warfare.

In Revelation, we have insight into the beginning of Satan's warfare, which was to eliminate the Christ child and the spreading of the Gospel:

> His tail swept a third of the stars out of the sky and flung them to the earth. The dragon stood in front of the woman who was about to give birth, so that he might devour the child the moment it was born. She gave birth to a son, a male child, who will rule the nations with an iron scepter. And her child was snatched up to God and to his throne. The woman fled into the desert to a place prepared by God, where she might be taken care of for 1,260 days. (Revelation 12:4-6)

These verses are flashes of truth without details or timeline. We know that the dragon is the devil, and the stars swept out of the sky are the angels who followed him. The woman is Mary and the male child is Jesus. Satan planned to have Jesus killed, but God found a safe refuge for the family. An angel appeared to Joseph in a dream telling him to take the family to Egypt, which was outside the dominion of King Herod, who planned to kill the Christ child. Jesus, being snatched up to God and His throne may refer to His anointing and God's protection after His birth. The number of days that are mentioned seem to be the time that the family was in Egypt and nearby areas to escape King Herod. They were in exile until Herod died. (Matthew 2)

This passage aligns with Herod's command that all male children in Bethlehem under the age of two be killed. This took place after Herod was told by the Magi of the birth of a child who was destined to be the King of the Jews. Herod believed that anyone claiming kingship over the Jews would destroy his dynasty. This bloodbath, known as the "Massacre of the Innocents," reveals Satan's evil intentions and influences from the day that Jesus was born. Judas' betrayal of Christ can also be understood in this context. Even today, Satan and his followers are bent upon destroying God's message of salvation.

John Wesley said that the devil's first work is to destroy the kingdom of God within us. One of his most effective weapons is planting doubt in the hearts and minds of people, a method that proved successful in the Garden of Eden. He mingles truth with falsehood in an effort to appear godly and concerned about our welfare. As the angel of light (II Corinthians 11:14), Satan strives to make things look good and right. He even convinces people that he does not exist and that evil is an illusion. Many people have been snared in this trap, and the numbers are growing. If Satan does not exist, there is no need for a Savior, and this is the final blow for those who have fallen prey to godlessness.

The question is not whether evil exists, for it is all around us. Our concern addresses the spiritual strength that is necessary to fight the many faces of evil in the world. This includes recognizing the latent forces that seek our destruction and prevent us from entering the kingdom. Years ago, I would never have imagined how quickly evil would spread throughout the world. All restraints have been removed, and the frightening truth is that many people are not aware of it.

## DEMONS

The primary work of demons is to extend Satan's mission, which is to spread evil and block God's saving grace. Although demonic possession is a reality, much of what we encounter relates to the influence of evil over people. Satan has started a fire that has spread throughout the world. He put the wheels in motion, and he observes the destruction. As the fire spreads, the evil recycles in its many forms. The sins of humanity are the cause of all manner of violence, including the wars that keep us on the fringe of annihilation.

Jesus believed in demons, and we know that He performed exorcisms. I have heard people say that the individuals encountered by Jesus were not demon possessed. Instead, they probably had epilepsy or another disorder. I'm certain that the Son of God knew the difference. If you read the exorcism accounts, you can come to your own conclusion. The Gospels state that many people came to Jesus to be healed. (Matthew 8:16; Luke 4:40-41) While some of these people had an illness or disorder, it is apparent that others were demon possessed. (Matthew 12:25-28, 17:14-20; Mark 1:23-27, 5:6-17, 9:14-29; Luke 9:37-43)

In the Gospel according to Mark we read about an unusual possession that involved multiple demons who were given permission by Jesus to enter pigs:

> They went across the lake to the region of Gerasenes. When Jesus got out of the boat, a man with an evil spirit

came from the tombs to meet him. This man lived in the tombs, and no one could bind him anymore, not even with a chain. He had often been chained hand and foot, but he tore the chains apart and broke the irons on his feet. No one was strong enough to subdue him. Night and day among the tombs and in the hills, he would cry out and cut himself with stones. When he saw Jesus from a distance, he ran and fell on his knees in front of him. He shouted at the top of his voice, "What do you want with me, Jesus, Son of the Most High God? Swear to God that you won't torture me!" For Jesus was saying to him, "Come out of this man, you evil spirit!" Then Jesus asked him, "What is your name?" "My name is Legion," he replied, "for we are many." And he begged Jesus again and again not to send them out of the area. (Mark 5:1-20)

What follows is a shocking occurrence. The demons begged Jesus to send them among a herd of about two thousand pigs that were on a nearby hillside. Jesus gave permission, and the evil spirits came out of the man and went into the pigs. The pigs then ran down a steep hill and into a lake where they drowned.

This man called himself Legion, because he was possessed by many evil spirits. During the time of Christ, a Roman army legion comprised at least three thousand men, however, it is doubtful that the man meant to use the word in this way. Instead, it was probably used to convey an unusually large number. This tortured man was living among the tombs, which were located outside the city. It was a place where criminals and outcasts often took refuge. The sepulchers afforded them both shelter and retreat from the weather and the authorities.

Humanly speaking, this was a hopeless situation, for there is no worldly power that can deliver someone from this overpowering torture. The man was controlled by multiple demons that gave him extraordinary strength. No restraint could subdue him, not even the chains locked around his hands and feet. He was out of control and a threat to both himself and others. The demons had taken over his life, and restoration was only possible through divine intervention and power.

The man saw Jesus from a distance, and he fell on his knees in front of him. The evil within him shuddered, knowing that Jesus had the power of expulsion. As in this situation, God's penetrating light sees the evil within every person, and He alone has the power to remove it. The demonic presence within the man asked, "What do you want with me, Jesus, Son of the Most High God?" This was a fearful response, for Jesus came into the world to confront every manner of evil.

Our Savior knows the hopelessness of those who are controlled by sin and how it impacts upon their lives and those around them. Evil can have such a grip on one's spirit that submission is sometimes the result. Resisting God's love opens the door to every manner of evil activity. Although the results are pain and despair, people continue to engage in sinful activities. We see this truth everywhere, along with the destruction that it causes. Jesus repeatedly warned the apostles and His followers about submitting to temptations. The Lord's Prayer directly speaks to temptation and the power of evil. In this brief prayer taught by Jesus are the words, *lead us not into temptation and deliver us from evil.*

Jesus rescued the man from demonic possession, which amazed onlookers. They asked each other, "What is this? A new teaching—and with authority! He even gives orders to evil spirits, and they obey him." This is the Jesus who is our Lord and Savior. He has the power to deliver everyone from the evil that seeks to control their life.

In the "Parable of the Weeds," Jesus told His disciples, "The one who sowed good seed is the Son of Man. The field is the world, and the good seed stands for the sons of the kingdom. The weeds are the sons of the evil one, and the enemy who sows them is the devil. The harvest is the end of the age, and the harvesters are angels." (Matthew 13:37-39)

In this illustration, Jesus again taught the existence of Satan and the destructive forces of evil. It also speaks to the judgment when Satan and his followers will be eternally punished. Although there is much speculation, we do not know why the Lord has allowed evil to spread to such an extent. We are assured, however, that one day evil will not exist for the righteous. Just as the wars between countries eventually cease, the Lord will bring our war with evil to an end.

The controversy surrounding demonic possession and the paranormal is seldom debated in seminaries and schools of theology, however, it is a topic that holds an interest for me. Both in parish ministry and the prison system, I encountered individuals and events that raised questions. I do not possess any special knowledge, but my studies, personal experiences, and the reports of other people, have provided insights that I will share.

**GOD'S ANGELS**

Many books have been written about angels, specifically how they glorify God and intercede on our behalf. The author of

Hebrews wrote that the number of angels in heaven are innumerable. (Hebrews 12:22) Angels are God's agents in the execution of His providence. Throughout the Scriptures we find angels involved in different activities, from making God's announcements to spiritual warfare. In fact, we learn that they will participate during the time of tribulation and the final judgment.

In addition to the archangel Michael, there are five types of angels mentioned in the Scriptures, which are: ruling angels (Ephesians 3:10), guardian angels (Matthew 18:10; Hebrews 1:14), seraphim who worship God and spread His glory (Isaiah 6:1-4), cherubim who echo God's holiness (Genesis 3:21-24), and elect angels. (I Timothy 5:21) The ministries of angels may extend beyond these particular categories. Angels were involved in every aspect of Jesus' life, including: announcing His birth, providing strength in the wilderness when He was tempted by the devil, in Gethsemane prior to His arrest, rolling away the stone of His sepulcher, and announcing His resurrection and ascension. We can be assured that there were angels who tended to Christ at the time of His resurrection. Since Jesus died a sinner's death, there is no mention of angels during His crucifixion.

In Hebrews we read, "Are not all angels ministering spirits sent to serve those who will inherit salvation?" (Hebrews 1:14) In the "Parable of Lazarus and the Rich Man," it was angels who carried Lazarus to Abraham's side. In the illustration of the "Lost Coin," Jesus said that the angels rejoice over every sinner who repents. Their ministry to humanity involves our prayers (Acts 12:7), encouragement in times of danger (Acts 27:23-24), involvement in evangelism (Luke 15:10; Acts 8:26), and providing peace to the faithful at the time of their death. (Luke 16:22; Jude 9)

I have often reported the peace experienced by parishioners at the time of their death.

In 1995, I was the chaplain for an execution. Not only did the inmate manifest peace, but the execution team spoke about a peace that they experienced. I wrote about this in my book *Ministry to the Incarcerated*, the highlights of which I will share in this writing. It was a day that impacted my life and ministries.

There are angels all around us who are interceding on our behalf, protecting us from danger, guiding us down a certain path, preparing the way for us in difficult situations, providing strength and comfort and, in many ways, saving us from self-destruction. The Holy Spirit, in conjunction with God's messengers, know every movement that we make. One might think that only the faithful receive this grace, but the Lord sends His messengers to everyone in accordance with His will. In fact, God's messengers are directly involved in leading people to Christ.

Like many people, I know that God's messengers have protected me over the years. Whether it was the motorcycle accident that I miraculously survived, the months that I spent on the flightdeck of an aircraft carrier, or the dangers of police work, the Lord's angels were hovering over me. For example, when returning home from a church meeting late one night I was shocked to see a vehicle coming toward me in my lane. Realizing that a head-on collision was within seconds, I quickly turned to the right and into a ditch alongside the road. Before I could react, my steering wheel—without me touching it—quickly turned to the left, bringing my car back onto the highway clear of the oncoming vehicle. It was as though someone was in my car taking control. This action was unquestionably divine intervention.

## THE PARANORMAL

I consider the paranormal as situations that are not explained in the Scriptures. Today, cameras are revealing mysteries that were previously not seen. This increase in unusual sightings has led to books, articles, television programs, and many forms of social media. These reports have resulted in endless unanswered questions. Is the government protecting what they know and possibly their involvement with experiments and activities?

When someone claims to have seen something unexplainable, it is always questionable. We struggle believing witnesses, unless we have had the same experience. In the final chapter I will speak to situations that have taken place in my life. After each occurrence, I questioned whether it really happened, and I am certain that other people respond in the same way. The paranormal challenges our senses and well-being. For example, how do these experiences affect the religious beliefs that are foundational to our understanding of life and death? Also, if there is life beyond this planet, what does it mean for humanity? While we may wish to deny paranormal activity, it remains an unexplained reality.

For those who believe the teachings of Christ, the presence of demons is normally accepted. This is not to say that all Christians acknowledge evil spirits. While many church communities believe in some manner of evil, they may not define it within the context of the Scriptures. What challenges our thinking are the manifestations that are not associated with biblical teachings. These sightings and activities take many forms, some of which are menacing.

To gain some understanding of demons and how they become active in the world, I offer two examples that were shared with me. Although demons are everywhere, they are clearly revealed when given an opportunity. The following cases substantiate this truth.

In 1985, I met an American citizen while I was traveling in Israel. After spending time with him, he asked my thoughts on the paranormal. Being a pastor, he probably assumed that I possessed insights that I could offer to him. He told me that he briefly became involved with cult activity. On one occasion, he attended an evening ritual in a desolate area where twelve individuals in black robes were gathered. During the ritual, these people were calling out, imploring Satan's presence.

To his surprise, he found himself joining in this chant, even though it frightened him. After a brief time, he felt extremely uncomfortable, and he left before the gathering had concluded. Upon returning home, he wondered how many people are involved in these groups and what they expect to gain from their beliefs and activities. He remembers feeling relieved that he was safe at home and removed from that particular evening. Feeling secure, he began to resume his daily activities, until his world was shaken by unexplainable events in his residence.

He told me that on three occasions over a period of several weeks, books on a living room shelf were propelled across the room with amazing force. During these events he saw a shadowy figure on the steps that led to his upstairs. Not willing to move, he remained in his rented home for several months, but fear eventually changed his mind. The evil did not follow him to his next residence, and he never told the landlord what had taken place.

The next case involved a seasoned Lutheran pastor who I met while serving as a summer park chaplain in Pennsylvania. There was an instant bond between us, which led to a trusting friendship.

I immediately realized that he was a very sensitive and spiritual person, who was committed to Christ and the Church. After getting together a few times, he shared an alarming story with me.

Being curious, he said that he purchased a Ouija board and began to experiment with it. After using it several times with no results, he stored it in his office. But it wasn't long before strange things began to occur. First, he felt that his personality was undergoing changes. This was followed by horrifying events that he could not control. He said that when he would begin to write something his hand would move without his effort or intention. During these times, he uncontrollably wrote profanities and words that were unintelligible.

After failed attempts to confront this situation, he turned to his denomination for help. Although he was embarrassed, he believed that he had no choice. After several sessions with other clergy, he was relieved of his torture. Obviously, he learned a lesson that changed his life and ministry. He knew for certain how evil seeks to control our lives.

Both of these examples involved temptation and testing the evil realm. This was enough to create an opening to an outside dimension. These individuals provided a spiritual path that enabled evil to move into their lives without resistance. Unknowingly, some people are drawn into the evil realm because of their lifestyle.

In addition to Satan and his demons, there are paranormal activities that cannot be explained. People know that they have seen or heard something, but there are no answers to these mysteries. In such cases, it should again be understood that evil takes many forms. After study and personal experiences, I have outlined my beliefs:

- To some extent, we retain the ability to exercise free will when we die.
- When a saved person dies, they are carried to *Paradise*, which is the realm of God. This truth has previously been stated.
- Through the exercise of free will, those who are destined for *Paradise* can choose to delay for reasons, such as:

1. The desire to observe family or friends for the last time
2. An attachment to a particular place
3. Unresolved matters
4. Empathy for grieving family members
5. To witness important family events
6. Desire to assure others that they are alive.

Years ago, I visited a retired pastor who was dying. Even though he was in a weakened state, he asked if I would take him for a short walk. I hesitated doing this, but his family encouraged me to do so. When I took hold of his hand, he said that he wanted to see nature and his surroundings for the last time. He was at peace with his imminent death, but there was sadness in his eyes. We may also be at peace concerning our death, but we still have an attachment to the only life that we have known.

- When the unsaved die they remain in a place designated by God while they await judgment. I do not believe that they are able to enter this dimension.

- There is the reality of lingering energy that can sometimes be visible in some form. Those who die suddenly or under extreme circumstances, such as victims of accidents, violence, and wars, can leave energy that imprints upon particular locations. It is common for these situations to occur on battlefields, military ships, and other such places.
- An individual's image may temporarily appear immediately after a traumatic death, possibly because they have yet to realize that they are dead. In these cases, the occurrence is brief.
- Demonic activity can appear in many forms, such as poltergeists and shadowy forms. They are intended to cause anxiety and fear. Like other supernatural activity, they are dependent upon energy. As such, they are limited in duration, space, and time.

The Lord has given us the defenses to protect us from all manner of evil, but this necessitates being grounded in God's Word and living in faith. Again, the disbelief in Satan, his demons and worldly followers, is the most powerful weapon that the devil has in his arsenal. In the Book of Job, we learn of Satan appearing before God, who asked, "Where have you come from?" Satan responded, "From roaming the earth and going back and forth in it." (Job 1:6-7) Since his fall from grace, Satan's mission is one of self-elevation, deception, lies, and the destruction of humanity.

— CHAPTER SEVEN —

# Affirmations of the Spirit World

## FIRST PARISH

After being ordained, I was interviewed and accepted into my first parish. Having served in law enforcement for almost twenty years and, only involved in part-time ministries, I felt the weight of the responsibility and challenges, which laid ahead. The church was located in a small country town in Pennsylvania. Although it was a conservative congregation, the people were warm and receptive. There were a large number of teenagers and young people, which is not the reality in many churches. It was a large and very active ministry with Sunday evening and midweek services. The church had a finished basement where youth services and Sunday school classes were held.

During my second year of ministry, strange events began to occur. It was my practice to spend time in the church on Saturday evenings for sermon preparation and prayer. This allowed me to be alone with my thoughts. Rather than draw attention, I always dimmed the sanctuary lights. My office was just off the sanctuary, which is where I did my preparation. To pray, I would go into the darkened sanctuary and altar area.

On several occasions while praying, three large sanctuary

ceiling fans activated. Then, within minutes I would hear music coming from the basement. The first time this happened I quickly turned on all the lights and walked through the church, checking the rooms and making certain that the doors were locked. As I approached the basement, the music suddenly stopped. Although I had no answers for this activity, I did not feel intimidated.

On two other Saturday evenings, the same thing occurred, and then the activities ceased. I did not mention these occurrences to anyone, primarily because of the anxiety that it would have caused some people. Whenever I thought about these incidents, church members who had died came to my mind. We had deceased saints, whose lives revolved around the activities of the church. Who knows? Maybe one or more of them came Saturday evening and stayed for the Sunday morning worship service. Three other incidents took place during this time, two involving church members and one that I experienced in the church parsonage. I was beginning to wonder what I would encounter next.

The second situation was during the day, and it involved a young woman who was a member of the church. I knew that she was a local librarian and not married, but I never had a conversation with her. When I would see her in church she was reserved and unassuming. On this particular day I was in the parsonage, which was about fifty feet from the church. I saw her enter the church through the basement door. Assuming that she wanted to see me about something, I walked over to the church and went into the sanctuary where my office was located.

As I opened the door to the sanctuary, I was shocked by what I saw. She was running frantically around the outer aisles of the sanctuary. I immediately noted that there was no one with her, nor was there anyone in the building who was a threat. Within seconds I called out to her, but she failed to respond. After a few minutes she stopped running and then told me that something evil was chasing her. When I attempted to obtain more information, she became emotional and quickly left the church.

I made several attempts to contact her without success. Weeks went by without her attending worship services. I did see her one last time in church, but we did not speak. I thought that she may have experienced a nervous breakdown. My intention was to suggest a professional service that may be able to help her. This is not to conclude that some manner of evil was not involved.

Several months passed without any unusual events in the church, but what happened next was beyond what I could imagine. It was clearly demonic and threatening, and it lasted about twenty minutes. It took place when our church was experiencing many changes. Our congregation began undergoing tremendous growth, which initiated plans for a building project. While this was exciting for the congregation, there were some church leaders who were voicing concerns about negative influences coming into our congregation. As I listened to them, they were assured that I would be vigilant. Being new to the ministry, I was not expecting to hear anything of this nature

This was the environment in the church when evil was manifested in the parsonage late on a Sunday evening. While resting on the living room sofa I heard heavy breathing. Looking around, there was nothing in the room except my German shepherd lying on the floor next to me. At first, I thought that he was making the noise, but I realized that was not the case. As the sound of breathing intensified, my shepherd became agitated and seemed to be searching for the source of the sound. Within minutes the breathing was close to me, and I began to feel numbness in my body. My dog was growling and crawling across the floor. Realizing that this was an evil entity, I started praying for protection and overcoming power. While praying, I was surprised that the presence was not moving away from me. I continued to implore the Lord for help, and eventually there was peace. Sensing this peace, my shepherd began to relax.

I pondered the circumstances that surrounded what happened. I certainly knew that I was not exempt from evil confrontations and attacks. But was there a reason why this occurred, and would there be subsequent incidents? I rejected the notion that someone new to our congregation had somehow spread evil amongst us. I did, however, think about our rapid growth in another way. I believe that this was a stark reminder that in the midst of Christian growth and joy there remains an evil that is intent upon becoming known.

Before leaving my first parish to become the chaplain at Rockview State Prison, our community was struck with an F-4 tornado. It missed the church by approximately two hundred feet, but the surrounding residential area was devastated. I later learned that the tornado was 1.5 miles wide and traveled nineteen miles before it dissipated. When the storm ended, there were eighty-nine deaths, one thousand injured, and over six hundred million dollars in damage. In our area, six people died and sixty others were injured. Our congregation lost two young girls, ages eleven and twelve, with many people injured and hospitalized.

On the evening of the storm, I was in the church office. At about 10:00 p.m. I heard strong winds and the sound of objects blowing around outside. This was followed by hail striking the windows and roof of the church. Within minutes the lights went out. I found my way to the basement and exited the building through the basement door. Upon entering the parsonage, I realized that the house lights were also out. My wife and daughter were sitting in the dark waiting for me. We believed that it was just a severe storm and decided to retire for the night, thinking that the lights would be back on by morning.

In the middle of the night there was a pounding on the parsonage door. It was a church member asking if I knew that there had been a tornado. Being unaware, he told me that the local community was devastated. He said that there were injured parishioners and that one of our children had died. He believed that the parents of the child were at the hospital where she had been taken. I immediately left for the hospital, which was about ten minutes away. When I arrived, I was led to a room where the parents were. They were in a state of shock, and when I entered the room the girl's mother grabbed me and started screaming uncontrollably. After a period of time, the parents decided to leave the hospital and gather with other family members. I later learned that the tornado removed their home from its foundation. The family heard a loud grinding sound and instantly ran toward the basement door. As they stood at the top of the basement steps the girl's father was holding his daughter's hand. As they started down the steps the house began to shift, and the winds caused the father to lose his grip on his daughter.

When I returned to the parsonage, I was told that another child was killed in the storm, and that we had about twenty people in hospitals. I made contact with the second child's mother and then attempted to visit as many of the injured as possible. When my district superintendent learned of the deaths and injuries, he sent another minister to spend time with me. He was a welcoming sight, for I could hardly stand up, and I was emotionally devastated.

Within days after the tornado, the father of one of the deceased girls was killed in a truck accident. The grief in our congregation was overwhelming. We had three funerals, and I wondered if we would ever emotionally recover. Although our worship services were now simply prayer gatherings, we made an effort to continue some manner of fellowship. Rather than withdraw in our grief, we needed one another for mutual support and encouragement.

About three months after the storm, I was called by the parents whose daughter was twelve years old. They seemed anxious to share something with me. Since their daughter's death they continued to attend church, and their home was rebuilt on the foundation that was left after the tornado. The parents told me that they recently saw their daughter. The girl's mother said that she was in the living room knitting and for some reason was drawn to the large picture window. When she looked, her daughter was standing in front of the window smiling and waving at her. Believing that she was imagining this, probably because she longed to see her daughter, she called to her husband who was in the kitchen. Without saying anything, she told him to look at the window. When he did, he also saw his daughter smiling. As they both observed her through the window, she suddenly disappeared from sight.

In the midst of their grief and pain the vision of their child provided healing and strengthened their faith. There is no pain greater than that of losing a child. My wife and I have family and friends who have lost children and, although time is a healer, there is always pain and emptiness. The Scriptures assure us that there is a special place in heaven for children. It is important that we not only pray for those who have lost a child, but we must be the Lord's instruments of comfort and encouragement.

**PRISON MINISTRY**

Serving as a chaplain in a large state prison is unlike any other ministry. Not only are you working in the midst of security regulations, which are sometimes ambiguous, but you are interacting with extreme segments of society. Inmates represent multiple cultures, and chaplains must be an impartial pastor to the entire population. This necessitates being approachable, patient, and understanding in an intense and angry environment. People are incarcerated for every imaginable crime, some of whom prey upon other inmates who are considered to be weak, such as the elderly and mentally challenged. This is the environment that I felt led to enter after my first parish. I knew that it would be challenging, as well as a learning and growing experience. Needless to say, I was not wrong.

It took considerable time to adjust to my new environment. At first, I felt that everyone was observing me, both inmates and staff. They were checking out the new kid on the block, and I was certainly aware of it. It was only when I began to develop friendships with the staff, visit cell blocks, and engage in conversations with inmates that I began to feel comfortable. Having spent many years in law enforcement, it was initially awkward and somewhat intimidating.

Within a matter of weeks, I realized that the word was spreading throughout the prison about my former career. In fact, I encountered an inmate that I had contact with when I was a detective. He could not believe that I was now a pastor. I also discovered that I knew a police officer who was incarcerated. I was waiting for the next surprise! Fortunately, my previous law enforcement career was a curiosity rather than a detriment.

The demands on prison chaplains are relentless. I was confronted with every conceivable situation. During my ministry, there was a riot that left a number of staff people injured. There were also many assaults and stabbings. One stabbing occurred just outside the chapel window as I was administering Holy Communion during a worship service. During my tenure, the prison housed approximately 2,300 inmates. Although there was a Catholic chaplain, our scheduled time off resulted in days that only one of us was in the prison. This sometimes created an impossible workload. There were always unexpected situations that needed to be resolved before the end of the day. In addition to being a pastor and program facilitator to the inmate population, staff would sometimes seek our counsel regarding a personal problem. Added to this was the amount of paperwork that is required in the prison system. Because of security concerns, every movement must be documented.

The prison forced me to see a different side of ministry. Sometimes I felt that I was on a battlefield tending to the wounded. Nonetheless, it was a time of emotional and spiritual growth that has changed my life. Although there were many encounters and incidents that I could share, I will only highlight demonic possessions and a state execution.

While most of my interactions with the prisoners were not remarkable, there were times when I was confronted with pure evil. One incident involved an inmate whom I believe was demon possessed. Realizing that mental illness is often interpreted as demonic possession, there is always a hesitancy when making distinctions. In this case, however, I stand firm on my belief.

I do not recall seeing this inmate at a worship service, but in a brief conversation with him near the chapel, he stated that he wanted to meet with me. Although this never materialized, I frequently noticed him when I was making my rounds. He had a habit of staring at me whenever I saw him, but he never initiated a conversation. But things changed when I received a telephone call from the supervisor of the restricted housing unit. I was told that this inmate was there for a misconduct violation, and that he wanted to speak with me. That same day I went to the restricted housing unit where approximately ninety inmates were isolated from the main population for behavioral violations.

As I stood in front of his cell, he approached with an ominous smile. After stating that he was glad to see me, he began complimenting me for my ministry and how much he respected me. He then sang a song of praise, which he had written to celebrate my work at the prison. After he finished this bizarre presentation, he looked at me and began screaming profanities and voicing his hatred for me. The inflections in his voice were continuously changing, and the anger he spewed was daunting. It was a horrifying experience that lasted about fifteen minutes. The officer who was observing this suggested that I exit the cell block. As I was leaving, I wondered what would have occurred if he had not been locked in a cell.

On another occasion, an inmate in the restricted housing unit told me that when he was released back into the main population that he was going to stab someone. He said that he needed a release from the anger that was built up inside of him. This man's voice and demeanor was pure evil. I immediately reported this to an administrator and was surprised to learn that within days he was released to the population. It was not long before his threat came true. The victim was stabbed near the heart, but he survived.

There was another inmate in the population who believed that he was possessed, but he said that he was unable to enter the chapel to see me. Whenever he came close to the building, he felt like he was on fire. He told me this as I was entering one of the cell blocks. I later heard that he also spoke to the Catholic chaplain, who told him that he did not perform exorcisms. It was questionable whether this inmate was simply seeking attention or if his claim was valid.

These situations, like others that I encountered, affirm the existence of evil. When people deny this reality, they are vulnerable to these forces. The theme in John Bunyan's *The Pilgrim's Progress* sets forth the struggle of our journey to heaven. He emphasized our spiritual warfare and how it appears in different forms. We travel a rocky road that has many obstacles and detours, which is why we need a divine road map and the full armor of Christ. Our strength and perseverance is in our faith, God's Word, and the indwelling presence of the Holy Spirit.

What follows is something that I could never have imagined. After seven years at the prison, I accepted a position at a local church. I welcomed the opportunity to return to a community parish. I knew that I would miss the inmates and the dynamics of prison ministry, however, I was ready to develop new friendships and to reconnect with other pastors. The change would also enable me to be more creative without the security restrictions of the prison environment.

Three months into my new ministry, I was contacted by the deputy superintendent for treatment at Rockview, asking if I would be willing to serve as the chaplain for an execution. Rockview was the site for executions in Pennsylvania, primarily because of its central location in the state. I was notified because my position at the prison had not yet been filled, and the fact that I was familiar with the staff and the execution process.

It was surprising to me that the appeals in this case had been terminated. During my chaplaincy we had drills with the electric chair whenever the governor signed a death warrant, but due to appeals, the executions did not occur. This is why I was surprised to learn that this execution was actually scheduled. Just prior to the scheduling, the electric chair was replaced with lethal injection. The execution, which was to occur within a matter of days, would be the first one in Pennsylvania in thirty-three years.

I immediately agreed to spend the last hours with the inmate, whose name was Keith Zettlemoyer. I learned that he was thirty-nine years old and had been incarcerated for fourteen years, twelve of which were on death row in another institution. He was convicted of killing a friend, but I was not concerned about the details. I knew that if anyone needed a pastor it was when they were facing death, especially in this situation. But I found myself with many questions, such as:

- How do you interact with someone who is about to be executed?
- How should I pray?
- Will any of his family members be present? If so, will I have an opportunity to speak with them?
- How should I approach the final minutes?
- What will be the lasting impact upon myself and the staff?
- How will the inmate population react to the execution?

After considerable prayer, I decided to allow Zettlemoyer to take the initiative, especially due to the limited time that we had together. It was important that he share his concerns, final thoughts, and anything that he wanted me to communicate to others, including his family. My intention was to be a compassionate presence and listener.

Keith was a Christian, who had an intense desire to be a witness of his faith at the time of his death. How could I fulfill his wish? On death row he was not permitted to attend worship services, and he only spoke briefly to chaplains. He never experienced Christian fellowship, where he could testify to his faith. He accepted Jesus Christ into his life while incarcerated, spending his time praying and reading the Scriptures. He told me that he decided to terminate the appeal process and to accept his punishment, being assured of God's forgiveness. Many inmates profess Christianity, but Keith manifested the heart of someone who was truly transformed. At one point, he even voiced his concern about the emotional state of the execution team. This amazed me!

On the day of execution, I spent eight hours with Zettlemoyer. As I approached his cell, he was cordial and said that he was glad that I was there. Keith emphasized how important it was for him to be with a pastor during this time. He said that he never had a minister or attended church. He then informed me that I would be his pastor until he was put to death. This was a chilling statement, affirming that he wanted me there until the end.

When conversing with Keith, I immediately sensed a peaceful presence. He was relaxed and knew what he wanted to discuss. We dialogued some of his theological questions, including his desire to die. He shared his life with me and his deep guilt and remorse. He initiated the singing of some hymns, which was followed by us sharing the Sacrament of Holy Communion. He said that the sacrament made him feel close to the Lord. As the day passed, he occasionally asked me for the time. He was scheduled to be executed at 10:00 p.m., and he wanted to be certain that we spoke about everything that concerned him. In attendance at the execution were correctional officers, the major of the guard, the deputy superintendent for treatment, a physician, myself, a representative from the governor's office, a state police officer, and medical technicians. According to policy, we did not see the medical technicians.

During my time with Keith, I experienced a peace and calm that seemed to engulf the area. I questioned what I was feeling, believing that it was possibly my imagination. I certainly did not want to manufacture something that was not a reality. As I thought about this, some of the staff said that they were experiencing the same thing. Not only was Zettlemoyer at peace, but we were sensing a presence that was bringing calm to us.

# In final hours, condemned man found peace

## Killer asks cleric, 'What will you say about this?'

Before they wheeled him into the death chamber, Keith Zettlemoyer stared up from his gurney, caught the minister's eye and posed a final question.

"What will you tell people about this?"

The question startled the Rev. Henry Covert, with whom Zettlemoyer just spent the past seven hours, the last seven hours of his life. Covert didn't know what to say.

Zettlemoyer's demise a year ago tomorrow transported the state into a new era of capital punishment. In its first execution since 1962, Pennsylvania unveiled its lethal injection procedure that fateful night.

Since then, the state has executed just one more prisoner. Gov. Tom Ridge has signed 44 death warrants now, and the capital punishment debate continues to crackle across the commonwealth.

Nationwide, discussion of capital punishment received a boost from the Oscar-winning movie "Dead Man Walking," which chronicled a nun's work with a condemned inmate coming to terms with his fate.

Covert detailed his behind-the-scenes conversations with Zettlemoyer at Rockview state prison. A portrait emerged of a man at peace with himself as he discussed God, guilt and murder.

*'I wasn't expecting a person who would be more concerned about others than his own death.'*
— THE REV. HENRY COVERT

Photo and article printed with permission of the *Patriot News*, 2020 Technology Parkway, Suite 300, Mechanicsburg, PA 17050-9412.

Shortly after 10:00 p.m., Keith was taken from his cell and strapped to a gurney. As I stood next to him, he looked up at me and asked, "What will you tell people about this night?" I was surprised at the question, and I responded by saying that it was the last thing on my mind. He then nodded, after which the officers pushed the gurney into the execution room. I followed behind the gurney, and after it was placed into position I silently prayed, and at 10:25 p.m. he was pronounced dead. He refused to have his family at his execution, stating that he wanted to spare them the pain of watching him die. He had a deep love for his family, but to see them at this time would have been unbearable.

After Zettlemoyer's death, I joined other staff as they gathered together to express their thoughts and feelings. It was a reflective time for everyone. The focus of our conversation was Keith's sense of peace and how it impacted us. How could there be peace and comfort at a place of execution, and why did everyone feel it? For me, it was unquestionably God's spirit bringing comfort to a child of faith as he approached his death and transition into the afterlife. Although I had previously experienced this with other people, what occurred that night was a strong message that God's forgiveness and love reaches the darkest places in life. The deputy superintendent, who was amazed at what transpired, asked if I would consider sharing my thoughts with particular church groups.

When the execution took place, my book *Ministry to the Incarcerated* was already edited and with a printer. I telephoned my editor informing her of the execution and asked if it were possible to include spiritual input from that night. She agreed, and with her assistance it was placed into the Afterword of the book. Keith always wanted to be a witness of his faith, especially at the time of his death. If you recall, he asked me what I would be telling people about his execution. I was not able to respond to him at that time, but his witness is now in bold print for everyone to read and share. The Lord granted his wish!

## SECOND PARISH

My second church was Saint Peter's United Church of Christ in State College, Pennsylvania, which was only about fifteen minutes from the prison. It was a small congregation that was comprised of mostly seniors. For years they struggled to maintain enough members to continue worship services. This was a drastic change for me, but I was intent upon making every effort to move the church forward. After several years, the church began to come alive with an increase in members and weekly visitors. Young families started attending, which meant that we now had children in the church. Programs were initiated that previously did not exist. We added a fellowship hall and finished the basement to accommodate the growth.

The people were excited, and we became a church family with hope for the future. The county prison was nearby, and with permission I brought several inmates to church. The people were initially hesitant, but it wasn't long before they embraced their new visitors. My wife and I were at this parish for almost ten years; during this time I officiated at more than forty funerals. Although this was expected given the age of most congregants, it was emotionally difficult. Because we were a close family, everyone experienced pain when someone died.

There was a gentleman in his late sixties who did not attend church when I started my ministry, but his entire family were

The Rev. Harry Covert stands outside St. Peter's United Church of Christ in Ferguson Township, where he has served for more than five years. The former Protestant chaplain at the State Correctional Institution at Rockview has seen the church's congregation quadruple in that time.

Photos and articles on pages 102 and 103 are printed with permission of the *Centre Daily Times*, 210 West Hamilton Avenue, #181, State College, PA 16801.

active members. He was a farmer who worked every day, including Sundays. When I visited him for the first time, I sensed that he had a warm personality. I also noticed how attentive he was when I spoke. Before I left the residence, he told me that I might see him in church, and it wasn't long before he began attending worship services with his family. It was wonderful to see them all

# Understanding Death & Resurrection

Pastor Dr. Harry Covert conducts Sunday services at St. Peter's United Church of Christ in State College.

## Former cop walking a less-worldly beat

*Harry Covert is an ex-detective who found preaching to be his true calling: In that vocation, he's gone from Rockview to St. Peter's*

FERGUSON TOWNSHIP — As a homicide detective, Harry Covert had a real knack for pulling people in.

As a preacher, it's still his strong suit.

For nearly the past six years, the 58-year-old policeman-turned-pastor has been rounding up people for St. Peter's United Church of Christ on West College Avenue.

Over that period of time, he has put the arm on literally dozens of folks, beckoning them to a congregation that, after 150 years in the business, is coming of age.

"I was house-hunting, and Harry's house was for sale," says Paul Hallacher, a two-year member of the red brick church next to Rider Auto.

"The day I went to look at it was a Sunday, and he had his collar on. He mentioned his church; we talked about it, and I started going," Hallacher recalled.

"I didn't buy his house, but he sold me something else that day. He changed my life."

Church members such as Hallacher credit Covert with re-energizing a congregation that, prior to his appointment as pastor, had fallen on hard times.

Fewer than 20 people were regularly attending St. Peter's when he started preaching there. Now Sunday services draw 70 or 80.

"He has built up our membership ... drawn in people who feel he is the answer to their needs," says St. Peter's Consistory President Tom Roush.

"He makes home contacts, and people come to our church. He just has that good connection. People like him."

Covert didn't start out to be a preacher. He started out to be a cop. He worked vice and homicide primarily, investigating cases for the Chester County District Attorney's office. Then, in his mid-30s, came

> "Coming to St. Peter's was a gift because the folks there reached out to me."
>
> **Harry Covert,**
> *pastor at St. Peter's Church of Christ*

the calling to the ministry.

He can't explain it; couldn't ignore it. He just did it.

And he did it the hard way, finishing three degrees — bachelor of theology, master of ministerial education and counseling, doctor of divinity — while working full time. He spent seven years in parish ministries, then, in 1988, became Protestant chaplain at the State Correctional Institution at Rockview. Seven years in that job burned him out, he says, and he took early retirement in January 1995.

Across town, the St. Peter's stalwarts were close to burn-out themselves. Their church, which never had a large membership or a fat treasury, by then, had gone three years with supply ministers and was on the brink of extinction, moneywise and memberwise.

Timingwise, the burn-outs could not have correlated more perfectly. Looking back on it, everybody now assumes the match was made in heaven.

"I had been offered an adjunct position at Penn State in sociology — administration of justice," Covert says. "We (at St. Peter's) worked out an arrangement where I could be their minister and still teach part time."

Covert signed on with St. Peter's first as a part-time pastor; he later took on the job full time. He still teaches at Penn State — courses with sobering names like violent crimes and correctional institutions and facilities. And he continues his outreach duties.

"He is visiting each family in the congregation," says Roush, "and, through that, we're seeing a marked increase in attendance. People have come back to church because of him."

Ironically, in May 1995, not quite five months after leaving the Rockview chaplaincy, Covert was called back to the prison to minister to convicted murderer Keith Zettlemoyer on the day Zettlemoyer was to die by lethal injection — the first inmate execution in Pennsylvania since 1962.

"I spent the last seven hours with him," Covert says, his voice lowering to a near-whisper. "When you go from homicide detective to a chaplain in that situation, you've gone from one end to the other of the process."

Covert was so moved by the experience that, following the execution, he went home and immediately put his feelings down on paper.

Through more providential happenstance, his book, "Ministry to the Incarcerated," was — on that day — at the printer's ready to be run off.

Alerted to what he had, Covert's publisher rushed the Zettlemoyer pages to the printer in time to have them added as an afterword to the book.

Covert is certain these things happen for a purpose.

"Coming to St. Peter's was a gift because the folks there reached out to me," he says. "After 20 years in the police department, then ministries, then Rockview, that was something I needed."

together, knowing how much happiness this brought to his wife and children.

As he continued to worship with us, I was told that he was diagnosed with cancer. Upon learning this I went to visit him. I could already see the physical changes that were taking place. Apparently, he unknowingly had the disease for some time. As his condition deteriorated, I visited more frequently, engaging him in conversation. When he lost his mobility, a hospital bed was set up in the living room. It was an emotional time for the family as they faced his imminent death.

It was not long before he passed away. I was not there when he died, but his wife told me that he saw deceased relatives standing at the foot of his bed. When I arrived at the residence, the family was waiting for me. We prayed together and discussed their desires for the funeral. I knew that his faith in Christ brought him into God's presence, and his family rejoiced over his love for the Lord. I prepared a service to celebrate his life, recalling his gentle spirit and how we drew close to one another during the previous months. I wanted the service to be personal, with words of comfort and encouragement for his family. It was a warm and meaningful service that centered on his faith and dedication as a family man. After the service and time of fellowship, I decided to give the family time alone. I visited with them a few days later to ask if there was anything more that the church could do.

When I returned home after the service I took my daily walk, which was a time of reflection for me. I pondered the brevity and uncertainty of life and how friendships can suddenly end. As I continued walking, I began to feel the pressure of warm air encircling me. It seemed different from the natural air that one would expect. At that moment I distinctly heard my friend's voice say, "That was really nice." After this brief statement, the air ceased, and the voice was gone. In amazement and wonder, I recall stopping for a few moments questioning what just occurred. I was astonished to think that his presence was in the church during the service that celebrated his life. From that day, I never viewed funeral services in the same way. He was in another dimension, but his spirit remained with us before the final journey to his heavenly home. When I told his family what had happened, they were overjoyed that his spirit was with them during their time of grief.

While at this parish, I became friendly with the Lutheran pastor whose church was directly across the street from ours. Robert was comfortable around people and very sociable. He spoke in a straightforward manner with a sense of humor. We shared worship services during Lent and special events. We would also meet for coffee or lunch when our schedules permitted. Since our services were at different times, I led the Lutheran services for him when he was on vacation. We shared many things in common, including our interest in sports cars. As our relationship grew, we openly shared with one another. Sometimes, he would call me late Saturday evening and talk about anything that was on his mind. He loved to tease people and solicit responses. He would often share his sermon material, asking what I thought as he was making his final preparations for Sunday. I appreciate down-to-earth honesty in a person, which is one reason why I enjoyed his company.

He and his wife had three adult daughters, one of whom was disabled and resided at home. The other two adult daughters lived independently. I admired both he and his wife for the care that they gave their challenged daughter. They left no stone unturned in making her happy and socially involved with the family. Robert's wife had a humble and kind spirit, and she was always there for her family's needs. Robert loved his family, often remarking that he was outnumbered by women who always had advice for him.

Sometime during the first five years of my ministry, I learned that one of Robert's daughters had cancer. Although I had not met her, I did hear about her successes and career. I don't know how long she was ill when I later learned of her death. Everyone was shocked and concerned for the family. Many of the people in my church knew her when she was growing up in the area. The funeral service was at the Lutheran church with our congregation involved. Sound equipment extended to our church so that we could be active participants. The attendance was in the hundreds, including many Lutheran clergy. After his daughter's death, Robert continued to pastor his church, but you could see the agony in his face. I could not imagine how he could be a pastor to others when he himself was in need of comfort. Losing a child is such a lonely road to travel. Robert shared his feelings with me, saying that it was only his faith that held him together. Although he tried to be positive, life became a struggle for him.

During my last year at the church, I was told that Robert was diagnosed with terminal cancer. I was devastated as I thought about ways to respond. As his health underwent a rapid decline, he decided to retire from the ministry. It was his only choice, as he no longer had the energy to continue. During this time, his disabled daughter became seriously ill, and she was hospitalized. I could not imagine what else could happen to this family. I spent more time with him, often sitting in his living room as he slept in a chair while receiving oxygen. By this time, he was continuously on oxygen and slept most of the day.

Prior to his death, I had conversations with his wife, who stated that Robert wanted me to preach his funeral sermon. At first, I was hesitant because of my emotions, but I could not refuse the request. The service was a supportive gathering of family and friends who knew his ministry to others, as well as his trials. I was honored to preach a message of hope, and to share my memories of him with those in attendance.

I have often thought about Robert, remembering both his humor and struggles, and how he continued to serve the Lord while carrying such a heavy burden. Although he was brokenhearted over his one daughter's disability and devastated when his other daughter died, he made every effort to be there for those in need. I certainly knew that he was with the Lord, but for some reason I began praying for him. I imagine that I wanted to hear some confirmation of him finally being at peace.

After a year, I decided to stop praying for a response or sign, realizing that nothing would occur. Then, while asleep in the middle of the night I heard a telephone ring. Thinking that it was the telephone on the bedroom nightstand, I sat up and immediately realized that the telephone was not ringing. I then laid my head back down, and I heard Robert's voice. In his usual manner, he called me by my nickname. With his humor, he had a certain way of saying it. After I heard my name, he then said, "You wouldn't believe it. I'm learning all about nature and creation." He then said, "Gotta go." I was stunned! Was he aware that I had been praying for him? Was he told to communicate with me?

After this brief but needed message, I never heard anything more. I knew that it would not happen again, which is normally the case in these situations. All I can say is that my prayers were answered. Robert had a painful earthly journey, but he kept the faith that carried him to his new home where he is at peace. I was also at peace, knowing that his journey was complete. I later heard that his disabled daughter died seven years after his death. Robert is now with both of his daughters.

**MY BROTHER'S SPIRIT**

My last experience was personal and family related. It involved my younger brother who died from cancer in 2016. Because of the age difference, we seldom did things together when we were young, however, later in life we became very close. Upon graduating from high school, I immediately enlisted in the Navy. After being discharged, my brother followed the same path. During this time, our lives went in different directions, and we only saw one another during family events and holidays. I became a police officer, and he entered the business and financial world. But after almost twenty years in law enforcement, I sensed a call into the ministry and began a long educational process. Since that time I seldom saw my brother, but this changed in the winter of 2006.

I was home recovering from my motorcycle accident when I received a telephone call. When I answered the phone, I heard someone crying and trying to speak at the same time. At first, I had no idea who it was until I heard my name. I then realized that it was my brother. As his emotions began to settle, he told me that his daughter had died. I knew that my niece struggled with drug addiction since her teenage years. My brother and his wife tried everything in an attempt to cure her of the disease, but they were not successful. Over the years I recall telephone calls with my brother when we spoke about her life and possible ways to help her.

My brother asked if I would participate in his daughter's funeral, which was being held at a church near Philadelphia. I assured him that my wife and I would arrive the day before the service. Like any parent who loses a child, the family was grieving and their emotions were shattered. My brother was a broken man, and he was never the same after her death. He always felt that there was one more thing that he could have done to save her life.

About seven years after his daughter's death, he was experiencing discomfort, and he underwent tests to determine the cause. The test results indicated that he needed open heart surgery. Although the surgery was successful, it was a slow recovery. He was experiencing back pain, which he attributed to aftereffects from his operation. As the pain persisted and intensified, his doctor ordered additional tests. It wasn't long before he was told that he had terminal cancer and six months to live. He attempted chemo, but he could not tolerate the treatments. He died after a two-week stay in the hospital. I later learned that the cancer had spread throughout his body.

After his daughter's death, my brother and I became very close. We saw each other more frequently and often spoke on the telephone. My wife and I also had overnight visits at his home. On two occasions, my brother and I stayed up into the next morning because he had questions about Jesus' teachings and the Christian life. I sensed an urgency with him in that he wanted to learn as much as possible. Although we were raised in a Christian family, myself and four siblings had drifted from our spiritual roots.

When my brother died, my wife and I were in Greece visiting friends and doing some sightseeing. Prior to leaving on our trip, I spoke to him on the telephone. I was uncomfortable traveling at this time, but my brother urged me to go, stating that he would be receiving chemo treatments. About two weeks into our trip my wife informed me of a dream that she had. She saw a vision of my brother that made her believe that he was either dying or had passed away. Although I did not experience anything unusual, I was concerned about his reactions to the chemo, and I felt the need to speak with him.

After several attempts to call his family, I finally connected with his son, who informed me that his father had just died. In fact, they were in the process of making funeral plans. I was stricken with grief, and extremely upset that I was not with him during his final days. His doctors never expected him to die so suddenly. It was impossible to obtain a flight home that would have enabled us to attend his funeral. His son's father-in law, who is a Lutheran pastor and a friend of mine, volunteered to lead my brother's service. I telephoned him from Greece to voice my appreciation for his kindness.

Upon returning home my intention was to visit my brother's wife and son, but it was difficult to get together due to the transitions that were taking place. We did, however, speak on the telephone. My wife and I had recently moved from a large property into a townhouse, and several times my brother said that he wanted to see our new residence and spend time with us. This, of course, did not happen due to his poor health. However, within a week of returning home from Greece, several events took place in our home, which I believe was my brother's spirit.

First, one evening my office door forcefully closed. We knew that this was impossible because there was no air circulating in the house, and all the windows were closed. Then, late one night as I was sitting in the living room reading, I heard my brother call my name. This was followed by a bright flash of light in front of me. After these occurrences I sensed his presence in the house for another day. Then, everything stopped, and I knew he was gone.

Since I was not able to be with him during the days leading up to his death, I believe that he willed to be in our home. In many cases it is difficult to know why these manifestations take place, but I am certain of the reason in this situation. Although I deeply miss him, I have joy in knowing that our conversations about the Lord were directed by God to help him on his journey. Even before he had cancer, I believe that he knew that he would soon die. The Lord gave us time together, which enabled my brother to understand the Gospel and to give his heart to Christ.

I do not profess to have any special gift or connection to the spirit world, but I believe that clergy sometimes have these experiences because of their sensitivity to the afterlife. A lifetime of ministry to dying individuals and their families may be a factor. I imagine that people in certain medical professions report similar situations. There is spiritual activity all around that is not openly manifested.

# Conclusion

In this book I have provided insight into the biblical understanding of death and resurrection, including the events that lead to the end of the age and the establishment of God's kingdom. Although the Scriptures do not provide details, we are given a road map, which emphasizes the urgency for us to be prepared. We have the promises of Jesus and the teachings of the apostles to guide us on our journey to the next world. We know that one day we will all stand before the Lord. For the unrepentant, it will be an accountability and judgment that will result in an eternal separation from God. The righteous, who have persevered in faith, are the heirs to God's eternal blessings.

Our journey to the next world involves obstacles and detours that make our travel difficult, including evil forces intent upon preventing us from reaching our destination. It is important, therefore, that we remain focused on Jesus and His promises. The apostle Paul compared life to a race that involves preparation, pain, and endurance. To finish the race, we must prayerfully persist until we cross the finish line. Time is of the essence, for no one is guaranteed another day

The writer and religious leader Joseph Fielding Smith wrote, "Everyone born into this world will die. It matters not where you are, or whether you are rich, powerful and educated, or among the poor and lowly in the world. Your days are numbered. In due time you will reach the end." He continued by emphasizing that we should all think about this, but not with a heavy heart. Smith was thankful for the knowledge that God provides through the teachings and resurrection of Jesus Christ. It gave him a peace that the world cannot take away. In his spirit he knew that in the midst of death there is life.

We must examine our lives in light of God's Word and the forgiving grace offered to us through our Savior. But any understanding gained through the Scriptures is fruitless unless we step out in faith and live a righteous life. Faith is the key that unlocks the door to understanding. It is through faith that God plans our life and accompanies us on our journey.

Jesus tells us that although many people know His name, they do not have a personal relationship with Him. To His disciples He said, "Not everyone who says to me, 'Lord, Lord,' will enter the kingdom of heaven, but only he who does the will of my Father who is in heaven. Many will say to me on that day, 'Lord, did we not prophesy in your name, and in your name drive out demons and perform many miracles?' Then I will say to them plainly, 'I never knew you. Away from me, you evil doers!'" (Matthew 7:21-23)

Kierkegaard lived a life of faith, but he struggled with the institutional church of his day. He contended that many professing Christians simply went through the motions. In his criticism of the state church, he wrote, "Jesus does not say admire me, worship me, or observe me. Instead, he says, come unto me." This requires faith and a changed heart.[12] Kierkegaard saw the Church as a house of illusions, in which many people were simply following the lead of others while neglecting a personal relationship with Christ. He wrote that Christianity is not centered on knowing the truth, but rather becoming the truth. Like Bonhoeffer, he believed that many Christians seek an undemanding spirituality.[13] In his book *The Cost of Discipleship*, Bonhoeffer called this cheap grace.

How we live our lives in the present determines our eternal destiny. Our earthly journey is not an easy path, but Jesus promises to never leave or forsake us. The indwelling presence of the Holy Spirit is offered to everyone who opens their heart in faith. We need not travel through this life alone! Paul said that when he is weak, it is then that he is strong. In other words, it was during his times of weakness and struggle that his faith opened the door to the powerful presence of Christ in his life. Let us take this earthly journey with the Lord at our side and His Spirit within us, knowing that our hope in Jesus Christ is certain. Like the Israelites, we do not know when we will reach the Promised Land, but with our love for God and His abiding grace, we will arrive.

Charles Kingsley was a priest of the Church of England, a university professor, social reformer, and novelist. He wrote, "Death is not death if it brings us nearer to Christ, who is the fount of life. Death is not death for those who live in Jesus Christ, for Jesus has conquered death for those who trust in him." Jesus

---

[12]  Clare Carlisle, *Philosopher of the Heart: The Restless Life of Soren Kierkegaard* (New York: Farrar, Straus, and Giroux, 2019), 9, 86.

[13]  Ibid., 74, 76, 220.

came not only to proclaim the coming of God's kingdom, but to give His life for its realization. Paul told the Corinthians, "Now we see but a poor reflection, then we shall see face to face. Now I know in part; then I shall know fully, even as I am fully known." (I Corinthians 13:12) One day the veil will be lifted, and we shall see the glory that awaits us. In Jesus we find a willing powerlessness. Even though He is the Son of God, He forfeited His divine power and glory, allowing Himself to suffer and die at the hands of sinful humanity. Rather than His omnipotence, it was His powerlessness that resulted in us receiving the kingdom of God. The suffering and death of Christ reveals the value of every person.

Many people have not had the benefit of growing up with a spiritual foundation. Although there is no guarantee that such a foundation will result in a relationship with God, it may lead to reflection at some point in one's life. Cultures throughout history have exercised the belief in a higher power to guide them. Their acknowledgment of one or more supreme beings has resulted in different responses and forms of worship. What is common among all cultures is the need for a power that is beyond themselves. This understanding has been given to them by the same God who speaks to us through our conscience and His Word.

When considering the many opportunities that we have to realize our need for God, it is surprising that so many people live without even thinking about their spiritual life and eternity. It is common for people to refrain from contemplating their death, primarily because it produces anxiety. People would rather see themselves in control and the master of their lives, rather than admit to needing a spiritual power. To acknowledge the need for God not only severs their pride, but it also speaks to their weaknesses.

Even those who consider the possibility of a higher power, may see themselves as "good people" who have nothing to fear. There are also individuals who do not comprehend what a relationship with God means and have no intention of knowing. Others proudly voice the rationale for their disbelief by saying that they adhere to science rather than a supreme being, or they remind us that a loving God would never allow human suffering. Instead of understanding that we live in a broken world resulting from sin, they blame God for humanity's ills.

These responses only strengthen our need for God. The suffering and challenges of this life are an affirmation that we need a spiritual presence and guide. Jesus encountered individuals who offered excuses why they could not follow Him. One man said that he needed to stay home to bury his father This sounds understandable, except that his father was not ill. Jesus knew that this was simply an excuse, and He responded to the man, saying, "Let the dead bury their own dead." In other words, let the spiritually dead bury their own. Like the excuse of this man, there are many reasons why people refuse to give their life to Christ. We must conclude, however, that they remain excuses. What is more important than one's soul and their eternal destiny?

We live in a fast-moving world of gadgets, technology, activities, entertainment, and instant gratification. All of these influences overshadow the need to examine our inner life. We have been consumed by a superficial world of constant noise, detracting us from what is most important. But instead of seeking God's

Word and the leading of the Holy Spirit, we look to this same world of deception and illusions for answers to our problems.

So, what is the answer to these destructive influences that are robbing us of God's grace; a life that is rooted in love and hope? The starting place is a prayerful examination of our inner life, asking the Lord to forgive our sins and to reveal what needs to be changed in our life. The results will open up an honest prayer life in which we are led to the teachings of Christ. Through our faith in Jesus, we will receive the Holy Spirit, who will bring discernment and guidance. This begins the journey to our heavenly home and to the light and glory of God's presence.

I conclude my thoughts with a writing titled *Jesus, Lover of My Soul*, which was written by Charles Wesley. It speaks of God's protective care as we journey to His safe haven, where He receives our soul:

> Jesus, lover of my soul, let me to thy bosom fly. While the nearer waters roll, while the tempest still is high, hide me, O my Savior, hide, till the storm of life is past. Safe into the haven guide, oh receive my soul at last. Other refuge have I none, hangs my hopeless soul on thee. Leave, ah! Leave me not alone. Still support and comfort me: All my trust on thee is stayed. All my help from thee I bring; cover my defenseless head with the shadow of thy wing.

# Final Thoughts

In his effort to strengthen the disciples by encouraging them to remain true to Christ, Paul wrote, "We must go through many hardships to enter the kingdom of God." (Acts 14:22) Jesus spoke about this when He said to His disciples, "In this world you will have trouble. But take heart! I have overcome the world." We were not promised carefree living, but we are promised strength to weather the storms. No one will escape the challenges and trials of this world. Jesus and His apostles certainly knew the suffering that precedes death. A clergy friend said, "You don't need to search for the desert because the desert will come to you." An unknown author wrote, "You never know that Jesus is all that you have, until He is all that you have." It is sad to think that so many people live without realizing these truths.

In one of his sermons, the Presbyterian pastor John Wilkes said, "Concerning pain and suffering, there is no way to shuffle the cards to deal it out. In the world you and I will experience tribulation. It may go around you for a while, but sooner or later it will go right through you." The country and folk singer Alison Kraus wrote a very moving song about faith in God during difficult times. These are some of the lyrics:

> *I've seen hard times, and I've been told there must be a reason for it all.*
> *Hurting brings my heart to you, crying with my needs, depending on your love to carry me; the love that shed blood for all the world to see.*
> *In all the things that cause me pain, you gave me eyes to see.*
> *I do believe, but help me with my unbelief.*
> *I've seen hard times and I've been told, there must be a reason for it all.*

Life is a paradox, for it can suddenly change from joy to sorrow in a matter of seconds. No one knows what is around the corner or over the next hill. Pastors are familiar with the trials and suffering of other people, sometimes ministering to them through their own pain. In fact, the compassion that we have for other people is often born out of our own painful experiences. Within this truth is the suffering of God, who not only suffers with us, but also because of us. In Jesus, the Shepherd became one of the sheep that He might experience human suffering and death. God has chosen to be in the midst of our pain. This is a love that is impossible to define!

It is not adversity that defines us, but rather how we respond to adversity. While some people are drawn to God for strength, others are consumed by anger. Napoleon Bonaparte said, "It requires more courage to suffer than to die." The English writer William Penn saw suffering in a different way when he wrote, "No pain—no palm, no thorns—no throne, no gall—no glory, no cross—no crown."

# Scripture References

**ANGELS**

Genesis 3:22-24; 18:1-2; 19:13
Job 38:6-7
Isaiah 6:1-3
Daniel 10:13, 21; 12:1
Matthew 2:13; 4:11; 13:39; 18:10; 26:53; 28:3,6; 12:25
Luke 1:26-33; 2:13; 15:10; 16:22; 20:36; 22:43
Acts 8:26; 12:7,23; 27:23-24
I Corinthians 4:9
Ephesians 3:10
I Timothy 5:21
Colossians 1:16
Hebrews 1:14; 12:22
II Peter 1:12; 2:11
Jude 6,9
Revelation 8,9,16; 14:6-7

**SATAN**

Genesis 3:14-15
Job 1
Isaiah 14:12-20
Ezekiel 28:11-19
Matthew 2:16; 4:1-11; 12:24; 13:39; 16:23; 25:41
Luke 8:12; 10:18; 11:18
John 8:44; 12:31; 13:27; 17:15
Acts 5:3
I Corinthians 7:5
II Corinthians 4:4; 6:15; 11:3,14; 12:7
Ephesians 2:2; 6:11-18
I Thessalonians 2:18; 3:8
I Timothy 3:6
II Timothy 2:26

**DEMONS**

Genesis 6:1-14
I Samuel 16:14
Daniel 4; 10:10-14
Matthew 4:24; 8:29; 9:32-33; 12:24; 17:15,18; 25:41
Mark 1:24; 5:13; 9:25
Luke 8:31; 13:11,16

Acts 5:16
II Corinthians 12:7
Ephesians 6:11-12
I Timothy 4:1-3
James 2:19
II Peter 2:4
Jude 6
Revelation 9:1-11; 16:13-16

## SECOND ADVENT OF CHRIST

Matthew 16:27; 24:3,27-31; 25:1-13,31-33
Mark 3:24-31; 14:62
Acts 1:11; 3:19-21
I Corinthians 15:20-24
I Thessalonians 1:10; 4:15-18
II Timothy 4:1
I Peter 5:4
I John 3:2
Jude 14-15
Revelation 1:7; 22:12

## RESURRECTION AND RAPTURE

Exodus 3:6
Psalm 23:4,6
Proverbs 14:32
Ecclesiastes 12:7
Luke 16:19-31; 20:38; 23:39-43
John 11:25-26; 14:1-7
Romans 8:38
I Corinthians 15:50-57
II Corinthians 5:1,8; 12:1-4
I Thessalonians 4:13-18
Philippians 1:21-23
Revelation 2:7; 6:9-10

## TRIALS AND SUFFERING

Psalm 18:1-2 (God is our rock, strength, deliverer, fortress, and stronghold)
Psalm 31:3 (our rock and fortress)
Psalm 46:1 (our refuge, strength, present help in trouble)
Psalm 55:22 (cast your burdens upon the Lord)
Psalm 61:1-2 (the rock that is higher than me)
Psalm 62:6-8 (rock, defense, strength, refuge)
Psalm 73:25-26 (the strength of my heart, my portion forever)
Proverbs 3:5 (trust in the Lord,

not in your understanding)
Isaiah 41:10-13 (I am with you always to strengthen you)
Matthew 5:7 (the merciful shall receive mercy)
John 14:27 (peace, let not your hearts be troubled)
John 15:7 (receiving through prayer)
John 16:33 (Jesus has overcome the world, victory in Christ)
Romans 5:3-5 (tribulation an instrument for personal growth)
Romans 8:17 (we are heirs when we suffer for Christ)
Romans 8:18 (present suffering not compared to future glory)
Romans 8:28 (all things work for good for those who love God)
Romans 8:35 (nothing can separate us from God's love)
II Corinthians 1:3-5 (God brings comfort to our suffering)
II Corinthians 6:4-5 (standing strong is a witness of faith)
II Corinthians 12:9-10 (God's grace is sufficient; trials enable us to experience the fullness of God's empowering grace)
Philippians 4:6-7 (let your requests be known to God)
Hebrews 4:16 (come boldly to the throne of grace)
James 5:10-11 (blessed are those who persevere)
I Peter 5:7 (cast all your cares upon God)

# Resources

Bonhoeffer, Dietrich. *Christ the Center.* San Francisco: Harper Collins Publishers, 1978.

Bonhoeffer, Dietrich. *The Cost of Discipleship.* New York: Macmillan Publishing Company, 1963.

Carlisle, Clare. *Philosopher of the Heart: The Restless Life of Soren Kierkegaard.* New York: Farrar, Straus, and Giroux, 2019.

Covert, Henry G. *Christian Beliefs and Prayers.* LaVergne, Tennessee: Lightning Source, Inc., 2010.

Covert, Henry G. *Discovering the Parables: An Inspirational Guide for Everyday Life.* Westport Connecticut and London: Praeger Publishing, 2008.

Covert, Henry G. *Spiritual Reflections: A Journey Through the Scriptures.* Westport, Connecticut and London: Praeger Publishing, 2008.

Metaxas, Eric. *Bonhoeffer Abridged: Pastor, Martyr, Prophet, Spy.* Nashville, Tennessee: Nelson Books, 2014.

Nave, Orville J., editor. *Nave's Topical Bible.* Milford: Mott Media, Inc., 1984.

Schlatter, Adolf. *Do We Know Jesus?* Grand Rapids, Michigan: Kregel Publications, 2005.

Unger, Merrill F. *Unger's Bible Dictionary.* Chicago: Moody Press, 1966.

Walsh, Sylvia. *Kierkegaard and Religion.* United Kingdom and New York: Cambridge University Press, 2018.

Young, Robert. *Young's Analytical Concordance to the Bible.* Grand Rapids, Michigan: William B. Eerdmans Publishing, 1964.

## MORE BY DR. HENRY G. COVERT

***Ministry to the Incarcerated***
Dr. Covert uses his experiences as both police officer and state prison chaplain to examine the environment of the incarcerated—people who are often forgotten by society. He emphasizes particular areas of inmate stress and how they impact upon the inmate's spiritual formation and the role of the Church in offering encouragement, healing and transformation. He calls for staff education, environmental improvement, and a pastoral presence that facilitates rehabilitation and hope, rather than discouragement and punishment. *(185pp. index. Masthof Press, 2022) $12.00*

***Prayers That God Hears***
The misconceptions relating to prayer make it a topic that is often abstract and difficult to understand. Dr. Covert's treatment of the subject is both biblically rooted and realistic. The simplicity of this book brings a clarity and continuity that is easily grasped and applied to one's life. It answers our questions and speaks to our deepest needs and struggles. This book is for everyone who seeks a meaningful relationship with God and others. *(140pp. Masthof Press, 2022) $12.00*

www.ingramcontent.com/pod-product-compliance
Lightning Source LLC
Chambersburg PA
CBHW070109080526
44586CB00013B/1245